A collection of

Machine Cuisine® recipes

featuring

nine menus and

more than 70 recipes

as taught at

Abby Cooks & Cooks & Cooks

Glencoe, Illinois

Machine Cuisine is a trademark of Abby Cooks & Cooks & Cooks, Glencoe, Illinois 60022

Sixth Printing, March 1980

Copyright © 1976, 1979 Abby Cooks & Cooks & Cooks
P.O. Box 118, Glencoe, Illinois 60022
Printed in the U.S.A.

Cover photograph by Fredric Stein.

ISBN 0-936662-02-6

Dear Friend and Fellow Cook:

Machine Cuisine® is my approach to quick creative cooking -- a concept that applies modern technology to recipe preparation.

With Machine Cuisine® techniques my recipes can be prepared in a fraction of the time they would take without a food processor and other time-saving kitchen equipment to do the tedious preliminary steps -- chopping, shredding, slicing, puréeing, mixing, kneading, etc.

The Machine Cuisine® recipes in this book are the same ones taught to my students -- professional and amateur cooks -- who attend my classes. They include a variety of appetizers, main dishes, salads, breads, sauces and desserts you may not have attempted before for lack of time.

I had fun creating the recipes and I hope you will enjoy using them.

Cordially,

Abby

Abby Mandel

CONTENTS

Useful Machine Cuisine® Techniques . . 1

Champagne Brunch 7

A Party Dinner 17

A Fish Dinner 29

A Greek Dinner 37

Picnic Fare 47

An Oriental Meal 57

An Indian Meal 65

A Parisian Dinner 75

A Scallop Dinner 87

Basic Recipes 99

Index 104

USEFUL MACHINE CUISINE® TECHNIQUES

WITH THE

CUISINART® FOOD PROCESSOR

STANDARD TOOLS THAT COME WITH THE MACHINE

Steel Knife: Chops, minces cooked and uncooked foods (including meat), nuts, cheeses; purées mixtures; blends and mixes sauces, spreads, pâtés, batters, doughs; kneads dough.

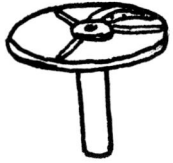

Medium Serrated Slicing Disk: Slices fruits and vegetables, sausage and cooked meat, partially frozen raw meat. Makes true julienne matchsticks of potatoes and other root vegetables, some cheeses.

Medium Shredding Disk: Grates or shreds cheeses and vegetables.

Plastic Knife: Mixes eggs, light batters, sauces, mashed potatoes (first shredded), dips, spreads.

USING THE STEEL KNIFE

The results obtained from this tool depend on the technique employed -- how many on/off turns to blend, mince, chop -- letting the machine run to mix, purée, knead -- dropping food through the feed tube with the machine running to mince small foods in small quantity such as 2 garlic cloves or a shallot.

On/off Method: This means a quick twist of the wrist in turning the machine on/off, done about as quickly as it takes to say on/off. The advantage is control, whether you are chopping an onion or cutting butter into flour for a pastry recipe. The Cuisinart® food processor works so fast that the contents of the bowl must be checked after 1 or 2 on/off turns to see if the desired results have been achieved. On/off does the work -- all you do is turn the cover. Always use a dry bowl and blade for satisfactory chopping or mincing.

All round fruits or vegetables must be quartered regardless of size. For example, peel, core, quarter an onion -- use on/off method with a twist of the wrist, checking after each turn to determine degree of fineness of chop. Chop 1 onion at a time unless very small (1 inch diameter). Do not overload the machine. Even if your recipe calls for 3 onions, minced, process 1 at a time. The results will be more uniform. Chop or mince apples, potatoes, beets, turnips the same way. Whether food is coarsely or finely chopped is regulated by the number of on/off turns.

Vegetables such as carrots, parsnips, celery, cucumbers must be cut in 1-inch chunks (always string the celery first) and seed the cucumbers to reduce liquid -- peeling is not necessary. Then on/off turns, watching carefully.

Mushrooms, after cleaning, should be chopped or minced -- 8 at a time, stem and all -- on/off turns until desired fineness.

Parsley leaves must be cut from the stems (done most quickly with kitchen scissors). Always use towel-dried parsley as well as a dry bowl and knife. Use on/off method until desired fineness. This is an exception to mincing in batches. The work bowl can be filled with parsley leaves and you will still have uniformly minced parsley. You can store the minced parsley in a plastic bag in the refrigerator for 12 days. If you are making a sauce, parsley leaves can be added to the mixture and will be minced as the sauce is processed.

To chop beef, lamb, veal, pork, ham, etc. -- cut in 1-inch cubes; process 1 rounded cupful at a time, on/off method, to desired texture. The Cuisinart food processor rejects gristle (a butcher's professional machine does not) which must be removed by hand after processing. <u>Note</u>: For an interesting meat loaf, chop each kind of meat (3 kinds are generally used) to a different texture...fine, coarse, coarser.

Except for Parmesan which should be processed at room temperature, all cheeses should be chilled, cut in 1-inch pieces, on/off method until desired fineness.

Chop nuts 1 cup at a time, on/off until desired fineness. If the nuts are to be ground very fine, as for a nut torte, use 1/4 cup flour from the specified amount in the recipe (not in addition to the required amount) to mix with the nuts when you put them in the bowl -- then let the machine run 30 seconds.

Lemon, orange, lime zest used in recipes with sugar can be quickly minced by placing peelings of the zest (use a vegetable peeler) and sugar in work bowl -- on/off method to get it started, then let machine run 60 seconds.

Let the machine run to purée any fruit or vegetable (first drain from syrup or sauce), to make bread crumbs and butters (herb or nut). On/off turns to get mixture started, then let machine run long enough for the desired result.

Flour Facts

Don't use more than 3 cups of flour in the work bowl. If the recipe calls for more, do it in several batches.

In mixing non-yeast cakes, breads and cookies, add dry ingredients after all the butter, sugar, wet ingredients have been blended together. Use on/off method -- stop instantly when last bit of flour disappears -- do not overprocess. If the machine runs longer than necessary, the baking results will be heavier.

For yeast dough, always proof the yeast. Mix it with warm water and sugar, or as recipe specifies, and let stand in warm place for 10 minutes or until a foam has developed.

Always measure flour with the "dip and sweep" method. Use a dry measuring cup with a handle and level it off with a spatula or straight-sided knife. Never add all the specified flour, but save 1/3 to be added only if necessary in the final kneading. After a ball of dough has formed and is of proper consistency (never wet, but usually sticky), knead dough letting the machine run, checking after 30 seconds to see if it is smooth.

<u>Important</u>: Never exceed 60 seconds in kneading. Do not worry if all the dough is not one cohesive ball. You can expect to find small pieces in the bottom of the bowl. Add these to the ball when you remove it. If your machine slows down with a sticky bread dough, add more flour to free the blade and get the machine running normally again.

Hint for slashing loaves of bread before baking -- use your <u>Steel Knife</u> rather than a razor or knife. It's far more effective.

With pâtes brisées (pie crusts), add dry ingredients to the work bowl first. Cut in the chilled butter and/or shortening with on/off method. Add the liquid through the feed tube while the machine is running -- stop immediately when mixture forms a ball to insure a flaky, tender crust.

USING THE MEDIUM SERRATED SLICING DISK

A wide range of slicing and julienning can be achieved with this tool <u>but</u> be sure to slice only what you would expect any sharp knife to slice manually -- known in the Machine Cuisine classes as the "knife test".

The results are achieved through various pressures that you apply with the plastic pusher after you have placed the ingredients in the feed tube. Whether you use <u>light</u>, <u>medium</u> or <u>firm</u> pressure depends on the softness or hardness of the <u>foods</u> to be sliced.

A <u>light pressure</u> is used, for example, to slice a peeled orange, whereas a <u>firm pressure</u> is required to slice an orange with the peel still on. Between light and firm, there is a <u>medium pressure</u>. This is used, for example, to slice a just-ripe apple.

Before you slice anything for your recipe, be sure you have first processed all the ingredients that need to be minced -- they need a dry bowl but sliced ingredients do not.

For a perfect slice, cut flat ends on your fruit or vegetable and be sure it does not extend higher than the feed tube (place the white pusher on your cutting board as a guide to length and width of foods to be sliced).

The feed tube is slightly larger at the bottom than at the top. You may find that a lemon or green pepper, for example, will fit through the bottom with ease whereas they might be too large to insert through the top. Therefore, before cutting anything in half to fit the top that looks best when whole, try inserting it from the bottom.

To slice large fruits and vegetables, such as cabbage, eggplant and pineapple, cut wedge-shaped pieces to fit in the feed tube, using the pusher as a size guide. This is the best way to slice these fruits and vegetables.

Cut cooked or raw meat in largest possible pieces that will fit in the feed tube, using the pusher as a size guide. Insert meat through the bottom of the feed tube. Cooked or leftover meat must be chilled to slice well. For best results, raw meat should be frozen on a baking sheet after being cut to size, then wrapped in an airtight plastic bag until ready to use. Defrost meat only until you can insert the point of a knife in it. The "knife test" again. Do not over defrost.

For a <u>true julienne or matchstick cut</u> (as opposed to what you obtain when using the shredder), cut any root vegetable, zucchini, cucumber, salami, cheese or slightly defrosted meat, etc. to the largest size that will fit in the feed tube from the bottom; slice once. Remove slices from the bowl. Hold cover sideways by the feed tube and insert the pusher, leaving a cup about 1 inch deep at the bottom of the feed tube. Stack slices in this cup so that they will be vertical when the cover is replaced on the bowl. Wedge in the last slice so they will not fall out when cover is replaced. Slice again. Repeat with remaining slices.

To be sure of getting round slices of carrots, celery, scallions, parsnips, etc., wedge them compactly in the feed tube to create a tight fit. First cut ingredients in equal lengths that will not extend beyond top of feed tube. You can also lay pieces of carrots, zucchini and other vegetables on their side in the feed tube and slice. This provides nice shapes for dips, casseroles, etc. If you are slicing a small quantity of carrots, for example -- cut the carrots in short lengths so there is a compact fit in the feed tube.

To slice small round vegetables such as radishes, olives and mushrooms for a garnish, cut flat ends and place them directly on the cutting disk in an area the size of the feed tube opening. It is too difficult to fit your fingers in the feed tube to arrange such small items. Put the bowl cover in place and use appropriate pressure on the pusher to slice.

When slicing small vegetables or fruits such as mushrooms, olives, strawberries, grapes, etc., start the build up directly on the slicing disk (cut flat ends for a secure balance). When the cover is replaced, additional vegetables or fruits can be added through the top of the feed tube. Remember to adjust your pressure to the texture of the food being sliced.

USING THE MEDIUM SHREDDING DISK

Whether the food to be shredded is placed in the feed tube vertically or horizontally determines the length of the shreds. Carrots placed vertically in the feed tube, then shredded will produce a typically grated result. The same carrots, cut in 2-1/2-inch lengths and placed horizontally in the feed tube, yield a longer shred, a kind of thin julienne.

The same "pressure" rules apply as for the serrated slicer -- <u>light</u> (always for cheese), <u>medium</u>, <u>firm pressure</u>, depending on the substance of the food to be shredded.

USING THE WHITE PLASTIC KNIFE

Of all the tools, this will be utilized least but it is indispensable for specific purposes -- for eggs, sauces, light batters, salad dressings, mashed potatoes (first shredded), dips and spreads -- especially when you want to retain some texture.

DOUBLE PROCESSING TRICKS

For finely cut coleslaw, do not shred the cabbage (there would be no texture). Slice first, then mince in batches with <u>Steel Knife</u> -- on/off turns.

To mince green pepper, slice with <u>Serrated Slicer</u>, then use <u>Steel Knife</u>; mince in batches, on/off turns.

To crumble soft cheeses such as feta, blue, Roquefort, slice first, well chilled, using <u>Serrated Slicer</u>. Insert <u>Steel Knife</u> -- on/off turns 2 or 3 times.

To mash cooked potatoes, shred first using the <u>Shredding Disk</u>, then mash with the <u>Plastic Knife</u>, on/off turns.

OPTIONAL FOOD PROCESSOR TOOLS

<u>Fine Serrated Slicing Disk</u>. This is similar to the slicing disk furnished with the food processor, but it cuts slices twice as thin. It cuts almost translucent slices of pepperoni and other hard sausages, and cuts cucumbers, mushrooms and other vegetables extra thin for salads.

<u>Fine Vegetable Slicing Disk</u>. This disk cuts slices to the same thickness as the disk described above. It is intended for vegetables only.

<u>Fine Shredding Disk</u>. This disk produces thinner shreds than the one provided with the food processor. It is excellent for shredded carrots and soft vegetables and cheeses.

<u>French Fry Cutter</u>. This disk cuts zucchini, potatoes, beets, turnips and other root vegetables into slightly curved sticks about 2 inches long and 1/4 inch thick.

SAFETY FIRST: ALWAYS

<u>Always</u> let the knife or disk stop spinning before removing the cover of the work bowl...<u>always</u> remove the <u>Steel Knife</u> before emptying the processed contents of the bowl...<u>always</u> keep your tools in a safe place.

SPECIAL NOTE

All Machine Cuisine® recipes are written in a specified sequence to minimize washing of the work bowl and other parts. So read each recipe through before starting to process the ingredients.

CHAMPAGNE BRUNCH

Gravlax, Mustard Mayonnaise

* * *

Baked Eggs and Cheese aux Herbes

* * *

French Brioche Bread

Fresh Strawberry Preserves

* * *

Crème de Camembert

* * *

German Apple Pancake

or

Fresh Peach and Blueberry Crêpes, Vanillées

* * *

Classic American Coffee Cake

GRAVLAX
(Swedish marinated salmon)

Its flavor is truer and more interesting than smoked salmon. Be sure to slice with a very sharp knife.

```
   1 cup dill sprigs, firmly packed or
 1/3 cup dried dill
   3 pounds fresh salmon, center cut
   2 tablespoons salt
 1/4 cup sugar
   2 tablespoons freshly ground white pepper
   2 tablespoons oil
   1 lemon, scored, ends cut off
   1 cucumber, scored, ends cut off, cut in
     4-inch lengths
  12 cherry tomatoes
     Fresh dill, parsley or watercress
```

Steel Knife: Drop dill sprigs through feed tube with machine running. Process until finely minced.

Cut salmon in half lengthwise into 2 equal pieces. For easy slicing, remove any remaining bones from salmon with a tweezer. Combine dill, salt, sugar and pepper. Brush oil on fish fillets, sprinkle dill mixture evenly over cut surfaces (not on skin). Place half of fish, skin side down, on large piece of foil. Place other fish half, skin side up, on top of bottom piece. Wrap entirely in foil; place in glass, enamel or stainless steel dish. Weight heavily with bricks, refrigerate 48 hours. Turn fish three times, unwrapping foil, basting with drawn juices and rewrapping with foil.

Serve within 5 days of initial preparation; scrape away dill, pat dry with paper towels. Slice thinly on diagonal, separating salmon from the skin. Arrange slices on platter. Serrated Slicer: Use firm, not hard, pressure to slice lemon (firm, thick-skinned lemons slice well). Use medium pressure to slice cucumber. Arrange lemon and cucumber slices on platter. Garnish with cherry tomatoes and sprigs of dill, parsley or watercress. Serve with Mustard Mayonnaise (recipe follows).

Makes 8 servings.

MUSTARD MAYONNAISE

- 1 USDA large egg
- 1 USDA large egg yolk
- 1 teaspoon salt
- 1 teaspoon red wine vinegar
- 1 teaspoon lemon juice
- 3 teaspoons Dijon mustard
- 1-1/2 cups oil (use your choice -- I use safflower with 3 tablespoons French olive oil)
- 1/2 cup whipping cream

Steel Knife: Place egg, egg yolk, salt, wine vinegar, lemon juice, mustard and 3 tablespoons oil in bowl. Process until mixed and slightly thickened. With machine running, pour oil in steady stream through feed tube. When mayonnaise is completed, add cream. Process only until well combined, about 5 seconds.

Makes 1-3/4 cups.

BAKED EGGS AND CHEESE AUX HERBES

A quick and easy dish, sure to appeal to quiche lovers. You can make it 4 or 5 hours ahead, but do not refrigerate before serving.

```
  3 slices thin bread, crusts removed
      (1-1/2 cups bread crumbs)
  3 green onions, cut in thirds
1/2 cup parsley leaves, firmly packed
  1 cup milk
3/4 cup water
1/4 pound Swiss cheese (1 cup shredded)
1/4 pound mozzarella cheese (1 cup shredded)
 10 slices bacon, well cooked
 12 USDA large eggs
1/2 teaspoon salt
  1 teaspoon Lawry's salt
  1 teaspoon chervil
  1 teaspoon freshly ground black pepper
  4 tablespoons butter
```

Steel Knife: Place bread, torn into pieces, green onions, parsley, in bowl; mince -- 6 quick on/off turns. Soak bread mixture in milk and water 5 minutes; strain, reserving both. Shredder: Shred cheeses, reserve. Steel Knife: Crumble bacon -- quick on/off turns. Plastic Blade: Add eggs, seasonings, 1/2 reserved liquid -- let machine run 10 seconds. Combine this with remaining liquid.

Heat butter in large skillet. Add eggs and scramble until very soft (not fully cooked, quite runny). Mix in soaked bread crumbs and 3/4 of cheese. Butter a 6-cup baking dish (soufflé or flan) which has also been sprinkled with a little shredded cheese. Add egg mixture. Spread remaining cheese over top, then sprinkle with chopped bacon. Bake in preheated 400 degree oven 30 minutes or until brown and puffy. This can be prepared for baking a few hours in advance, but not refrigerated.

Makes 8 servings.

FRENCH BRIOCHE BREAD

Easier to make and lower in calories than the usual French brioche, but with true brioche flavor.

Glaze

- 1 USDA large egg
- 1/2 teaspoon salt

- 1 package active dry yeast
- 1/2 cup warm water (105 to 115 degrees)
- 2 teaspoons sugar
- 2-1/4 cups unbleached all-purpose flour
- 1-1/2 teaspoons salt
- 1 stick frozen butter, cut in 8 pieces
- 2 USDA large eggs

Plastic Knife: Mix egg and salt for glaze -- 6 on/off turns. Set aside, covered and refrigerated.

Proof yeast in warm water with 1 teaspoon sugar. Steel Knife: Place flour, salt, 1 teaspoon sugar and butter in bowl -- turn machine on/off until mixture resembles coarse meal. Add proofed yeast in 2 batches with on/off motion. Add eggs; blend thoroughly.

Let dough rise until doubled (about 2 hours) in warm place in oiled bowl, covered with damp cloth. Stir down, cover, refrigerate overnight or at least 4 hours. Form into loaf and place in buttered 9- or 10-inch loaf pan or 6-cup brioche mold. Cover with damp cloth, allow to double again (about 2 to 2-1/2 hours).

Brush on glaze very carefully without dripping onto pan. Bake in preheated 400 degree oven for 15 minutes, then 25 minutes more at 350 degrees or until sufficiently browned.

Makes one 9- or 10-inch loaf or 6-cup mold.

FRESH STRAWBERRY PRESERVES

Truer strawberry flavor than cooked preserves.

    4 cups whole strawberries (2-1/2 cups sliced)
    4 cups sugar
    2 tablespoons lemon juice
      Zest of 1 lemon
1/2 bottle Certo fruit pectin

Wash berries, allow to dry; hull. <u>Serrated Slicer</u>: Slice strawberries (stack in feed tube, apply gentle pressure). Place in bowl, add sugar; mix very well, let stand 10 minutes. Combine juice, zest and pectin in small bowl; add to strawberries, stir 3 minutes.

Pour preserves into prepared jars or containers. Cover so they are airtight and allow to stand at room temperature about 24 hours. Store in refrigerator up to 3 weeks or freeze for longer storage.

Makes 4 cups.

CREME DE CAMEMBERT

Milder and more subtle than Camembert alone. It spreads more easily and has just the right consistency to shape into a pleasing presentation.

    1 ripe Camembert cheese (8 ounces)
    3/4 cup dry white wine (Macon Blanc)
    1/3 cup unsalted butter, softened
    2 slices toast, crusts removed

Scrape skin off Camembert; place cheese in small bowl, add wine (enough to cover) and let stand at room temperature, covered, 12 hours. Drain well.

<u>Steel Knife</u>: Make crumbs from toast, cut into quarters, with quick on/off turns. Set aside; wipe out bowl with paper towel. Place softened butter and marinated cheese in bowl; blend until smooth, about 5 seconds.

Mold mixture in small bowl lined with plastic wrap. Refrigerate 1 hour, unmold; press crumbs into surface. Chill well before serving.

Makes 1-1/8 cups.

GERMAN APPLE PANCAKE

Batter

```
  4 USDA large eggs
1/2 cup unbleached all-purpose flour
1/2 teaspoon baking powder
  1 tablespoon sugar
    Pinch salt
  1 cup milk
  1 teaspoon vanilla extract
  2 tablespoons melted butter
1/8 teaspoon freshly grated nutmeg
```

Fruit Mixture

```
  4 tablespoons (1/2 stick) unsalted butter
1/2 cup sugar
1/2 teaspoon cinnamon
1/8 teaspoon freshly grated nutmeg
  1 large tart apple (Granny Smith, Greening), halved,
    cored, not necessary to peel (1 cup sliced)
```

Batter. Plastic Knife: Blend eggs, flour, baking powder, sugar and salt -- 6 on/off turns. With machine running, add milk gradually through feed tube. Add vanilla, melted butter, nutmeg -- 3 on/off turns to blend. Let stand 30 minutes at room temperature or overnight.

Fruit Mixture. In 10-inch ovenproof skillet, melt butter, brush up on sides of pan. Sprinkle 1/4 cup sugar, cinnamon and nutmeg over butter. Serrated Slicer: Slice apple halves, stacking them vertically in feed tube. Spread apple slices in even layer in prepared pan. Sprinkle remaining 1/4 cup sugar over apples. Place over medium high heat only until mixture bubbles. Pour batter gently over apples. Place in preheated 425 degree oven for 15 minutes, reduce oven to 375 degrees and bake 10 minutes. Slide onto serving platter; cut into wedges.

Makes 3 to 4 servings.

FRESH PEACH AND BLUEBERRY CREPES

The weight conscious can substitute yogurt for sour cream in the Vanilla Sauce.

Crêpes -- (25 5-inch crêpes with dip method)

- 1 cup unbleached all-purpose flour, unsifted
- 2 tablespoons sugar
  Pinch salt
- 2 eggs
- 1 cup liquid (1 tablespoon vanilla, 2 tablespoons Grand Marnier, 1/4 cup water and enough milk to make 1 cup liquid)
- 1 tablespoon oil

   Note: Increase milk to make 1-1/3 cups liquid for conventional crêpe pan. Makes 30 5-inch crêpes.

Peach Filling

- 6 large peaches, halved, pitted, not necessary to peel (4 cups slices)
- 3 tablespoons Grand Marnier
- 5 tablespoons sugar (or to taste)
- 1/2 cup blueberries (optional)
- 3 tablespoons orange juice
  Zest of 1 orange

Crêpes. Plastic Blade: Place dry ingredients in bowl, add eggs. Turn machine on/off twice. Add 1/2 the liquid, process 2 seconds; add remaining liquid and oil. Mix thoroughly. Strain, if necessary, to remove any lumps. Let batter rest 1 hour or overnight, covered and refrigerated. Crêpe batter should be like heavy cream. Add extra liquid if necessary. Cook crêpes on one side only. If cooked in advance, place parchment paper or plastic wrap between each, wrap in an airtight plastic bag and refrigerate up to 4 days or freeze for longer storage.

Filling. Serrated Slicer: Slice peaches. Place in bowl, add remaining ingredients and let stand 15 minutes. Place spoonful of marinated peaches off center of each crêpe; fold in quarters, arrange in well-buttered shallow ovenproof dish. Spoon marinade over crêpes. Bake in preheated 400 degree oven for 10 minutes. Sprinkle with confectioners sugar; broil, watching carefully. Serve with Vanilla Sauce or Crème Fraîche Sauce (see basic recipes).

Makes 8 servings.

CLASSIC AMERICAN COFFEE CAKE

I always have this coffee cake on hand for house guests so they can slice a piece en passant, as it were. It's a moist cake that keeps well, if you can keep it hidden.

- 1-1/2 cups sour cream
- 1-1/2 teaspoons baking soda
- 3/4 cup walnuts
- 1/2 cup sugar
- 2 teaspoons cinnamon
- 1-1/4 cups sugar
- 1/2 pound (2 sticks) unsalted butter, cut in 4 pieces
- 3 USDA large eggs
- 2 teaspoons vanilla
- 1 tablespoon rum
- 3 cups unbleached all-purpose flour
- 2 teaspoons baking powder
- 1-1/2 teaspoons salt

Combine sour cream and baking soda; let stand at room temperature 1/2 hour. <u>Steel Knife</u>: Place walnuts, sugar, cinnamon in bowl -- 4 quick on/off turns. Nuts should be coarsely chopped. Set aside. Mix sugar and butter, letting machine run until mixture forms a ball. Add eggs, vanilla, rum, sour cream. Let machine run 10 seconds or until mixture is well blended. Add flour, baking powder, salt. Turn machine on/off only until flour is incorporated.

Butter generously a 10-cup Bundt pan. Cover bottom of pan with thin layer of batter; cover with 1/3 of nut mixture. Add another layer of batter, then all of nut mixture. Spread remaining batter over all. Bake in preheated 350 degree oven 1 hour. Let stand out of oven in pan 5 minutes; invert pan, remove cake and let cool on wire rack.

Makes 12 servings.

A PARTY DINNER

Marinated Scallops, Green Mayonnaise

or

Tapenade, Crudités

* * *

Stuffed Breast of Veal

Herbed Tomatoes

Courgettes Rapées

* * *

Mushroom Endive Salad

* * *

French Bread

* * *

Tarte Tatin, Sauce Vanille

MARINATED SCALLOPS, GREEN MAYONNAISE

Your guests will be impressed with the sensational flavor of these scallops. The "cooked" appearance comes from marinating several hours or overnight.

Scallops

    2 pounds baby or large scallops, quartered
1/2 cup parsley leaves, firmly packed
    1 lime, scored, ends cut off
    2 shallots, peeled
1/2 cup fresh lime juice
1/4 cup water

Green Mayonnaise

    1 USDA large egg
    2 teaspoons Dijon mustard
    1 teaspoon fresh lemon juice
1/2 teaspoon salt
1/2 teaspoon red wine vinegar
1/2 cup watercress leaves, firmly packed
1/2 cup parsley leaves, firmly packed
1-1/2 cups oil
    Freshly ground black pepper

    Bibb lettuce

Wash and drain scallops well; pat dry with paper towels. <u>Steel Knife</u>: Mince parsley -- quick on/off turns. Remove and set aside. <u>Serrated Slicer</u>: Slice lime with firm, not hard, pressure. Refrigerate minced parsley and lime slices in plastic bags. Dry bowl with paper towel. <u>Steel Knife</u>: Mince shallots -- with machine running, drop in through feed tube. In a bowl large enough for scallops, combine chopped shallots, lime juice and water. Add scallops, mix well, cover and refrigerate until scallops appear cooked and whitened, about 3 hours or overnight.

<u>Steel Knife</u>: Add egg, mustard, lemon juice, salt, vinegar, watercress, parsley, 3 tablespoons oil and pepper. Turn machine on/off 2 seconds or until mixed and slightly thickened. With machine running, pour oil in steady stream through feed tube. Add watercress and parsley, both washed and well dried; turn on machine and let run until minced and blended into mayonnaise. Taste for seasoning, make necessary adjustments (be careful -- scallops are slightly tart).

Drain scallops thoroughly. Place in a bowl, mix in 1 cup Green Mayonnaise, check seasoning. Present on Bibb lettuce leaves. Garnish with reserved lime slices and parsley.

Makes 8 servings.

TAPENADE

Green peppercorns impart the piquant flavor to this quickly prepared appetizer. It will keep in the refrigerator for two weeks.

```
   1 hard-cooked egg, peeled, quartered
 1/8 cup parsley leaves, firmly packed
   1 clove garlic, peeled
   1 small onion, peeled, quartered
   1 can (7 ounces) Italian tuna, drained
   6 sardines, drained
 1/2 cup pitted black olives
 1/2 cup Calamata olives, pitted
 1/2 cup parsley leaves, firmly packed
 1/4 cup Tahini sesame paste
   4 tablespoons fresh lemon juice
     Zest of 1 lemon
   2 tablespoons capers, drained
   2 tablespoons anchovy paste
   1 teaspoon green peppercorns, drained*
   1 teaspoon thyme
     Freshly ground black pepper
```

Steel Knife: Chop egg and 1/8 cup parsley leaves together -- quick on/off turns. Refrigerate wrapped in plastic. Mince garlic; add onion and mince, turning machine on/off quickly. Add remaining ingredients, blending at first with quick on/off turns, then letting machine run until mixture is perfectly blended. Check seasoning. Garnish with reserved egg-parsley mixture. Serve with celery and carrot sticks, cucumber and zucchini slices, cauliflower and broccoli flowerets, etc.

*The canned green peppercorns are better than the freeze dried, but avoid those with citric acid. It denatures the taste. The best are those packed in water or brine. Otherwise get the ones in vinegar.

Makes about 2 cups.

HERBED TOMATOES

Another favorite! Enjoy them as either a vegetable or as a garnish.

```
  8 firm slightly underripe medium tomatoes
  6 tablespoons butter
  2 tablespoons light brown sugar
1/2 teaspoon salt
    Freshly ground black pepper
  1 teaspoon celery seed
  1 teaspoon MSG (optional)
  1 teaspoon oregano
1/4 cup parsley leaves, firmly packed
  3 scallions, cut in thirds
  2 celery stalks, cut in thirds
```

Place a few tomatoes at a time briefly in boiling water, then hold under cold running water to stop cooking process. Remove peel with sharp knife, removing the stem first. In a skillet large enough to hold tomatoes, melt butter -- add sugar, seasonings; mix well.

Steel Knife: Mince parsley, scallions, celery together -- quick on/off turns. Add vegetables to butter mixture, but only heat through -- do not overcook. Place tomatoes stem side down, spoon herbed mixture over each. Heat gently, basting a few times with butter mixture. These can be made in advance and reheated carefully. Serve tomatoes surrounding zucchini.

Makes 6 to 8 servings.

STUFFED BREAST OF VEAL

This veal recipe is demonstrably more economical than most. It does not require prime veal, and the romaine in the stuffing provides a distinctive taste.

Stuffing

```
  3/4 cup parsley leaves, firmly packed
1-1/3 slices bread (1 cup bread crumbs)
    2 cloves garlic, peeled
    1 medium onion, peeled, quartered
    3 tablespoons water
    1 tablespoon butter
    2 eggs
  1/4 cup Cognac
    1 teaspoon dried basil
    1 to 2 teaspoons salt
      Freshly ground black pepper
    1 pound veal meat from leg (1/4 pound can be
      pork), cut in 1-1/2 inch cubes
    4 ounces romaine (1/2 small head -- 2 cups sliced)
```

Veal Breast

```
    1 veal breast (4 to 5 pounds) (ask butcher to bone and make pocket for
      roasting -- request the bones)
      Salt
      Freshly ground black pepper
    2 tablespoons butter
    2 tablespoons oil
    1 clove garlic, peeled
    1 bay leaf
    1 cup veal stock or chicken broth
1-1/2 cups dry white wine or dry vermouth
    1 medium onion (3/4 cup sliced)
    1 medium carrot (3/4 cup sliced)
      Lemon wedges
```

Steel Knife: Mince parsley -- quick on/off turns. Remove 1/4 cup and refrigerate in plastic bag for garnish. Add bread, torn into pieces -- quick on/off turns until finely chopped. Set aside. Shredder: Shred garlic and onion; cook in water and butter until water is evaporated. Steel Knife: Return parsley, crumbs, garlic and onion to bowl. Add eggs, Cognac, basil, salt and pepper -- turn on/off only until mixture is blended. Remove to large bowl. Chop meat, keeping texture somewhat coarse -- quick on/off turns. Serrated Slicer: Cut romaine lengthwise to fit feed tube, slice, using light pressure. Combine meat with mixture in bowl, mixing well. Lightly mix in romaine. Check taste by sautéeing a small amount until well cooked, adjust seasoning as necessary.

(continued on other side)

STUFFED BREAST OF VEAL (cont.)

Salt and pepper pocket of veal. Stuff (do not overstuff), truss as necessary. Season exterior of meat with salt and pepper; brown on all sides in butter and oil. In a close-fitting roasting pan or casserole, place meat and bones, garlic, bay leaf, veal stock and wine. <u>Serrated Slicer</u>: Slice onion and carrot -- medium pressure, add to pan.

Roast in preheated 350 degree oven, covered for 2 hours, then uncovered for remaining 1/2 to 1 hour or until tender, basting occasionally and keeping vegetables submerged in liquid to prevent burning.

Remove meat to warm platter, skim off fat and any extraneous matter. Reduce sauce to desired thickness. <u>Steel Knife</u>: Purée sauce in batches. Place back in pan, reheat, check seasoning -- more wine can be added if desired. Remove trussing, slice meat, garnish platter with lemon wedges and reserved parsley. Serve with sauce. Stuffing can be prepared in advance, refrigerated. This dish is also excellent served cold.

Makes 6 servings.

COURGETTES RAPEES
(a shredded zucchini dish)

Quickly prepared and delicious.

   1/2 cup parsley, firmly packed
     1 clove garlic, peeled
   1/2 small onion, peeled, cut in 2 pieces
      (1/8 cup minced)
2-1/2 pounds zucchini, cut in 2-inch pieces
     2 tablespoons butter
     2 tablespoons oil
       Juice of 1 lemon
     1 teaspoon salt
       Freshly ground black pepper

Steel Knife: Mince parsley -- quick on/off turns. Remove and set aside. Mince garlic; add onion and mince -- on/off turns. Remove and set aside. Shredder: Stack zucchini pieces horizontally in feed tube. Apply medium pressure to shred. Repeat until all zucchini is shredded.

Heat butter and oil in skillet; add onion and garlic, cook 2 minutes. Add zucchini. Cook quickly, about 3 minutes, shaking pan occasionally. Add lemon juice, salt, pepper. Mix well -- adjust seasoning. Garnish with reserved parsley. Serve immediately.

Makes 6 servings.

MUSHROOM ENDIVE SALAD

An interesting fresh vegetable salad...high in food value, low in calories and pleasing in texture.

Salad

2/3 cup parsley leaves, firmly packed
12 large mushrooms
3 heads Belgian endive or
1 head Boston lettuce

Vinaigrette Dressing

3/4 cup oil
1/4 cup red wine vinegar
1 teaspoon salt
Freshly ground black pepper

Steel Knife: Mince parsley -- on/off turns, set aside. Serrated Slicer: Wipe mushrooms clean with damp paper towel. Slice mushrooms, using light pressure on pusher. Combine mushroom slices and endive, cut in halves, or lettuce, torn into pieces.

Mix together oil, vinegar, salt and pepper; pour over salad and toss to coat ingredients. Taste and adjust seasoning. Garnish with minced parsley.

Makes 6 servings.

LA TARTE TATIN

Tradition has it that two sisters -- the Mesdemoiselles Tatin -- created this dessert for their restaurant. It ranks with the most famous classical French recipes, and for good reason.

Pâte Brisée

- 1-1/2 cups unbleached all-purpose flour
- 1 tablespoon sugar
- Pinch salt
- 4 ounces (1 stick) chilled unsalted butter, cut in 4 pieces
- 2 tablespoons chilled vegetable shortening
- 1/3 cup ice water

Apple Mixture

- 6 large apples (Greenings, Granny Smith) (6 cups sliced apples)
- 1 tablespoon lemon juice <u>or</u>
- 1 500 mg. vitamin C tablet
- 3/4 cup plus 1 tablespoon sugar
- 3 tablespoons water
- 1 tablespoon lemon juice
- 1/4 teaspoon nutmeg
- 1/2 teaspoon cinnamon
- 1 teaspoon lemon zest
- 2 tablespoons unsalted butter

Glaze

- 1/3 cup apricot preserves
- 1 tablespoon Cognac
- 1 tablespoon water

Sauce

- 1 cup sour cream
- 3 to 4 tablespoons Greek vanilla syrup*

<u>Pâte Brisée</u>. <u>Steel Knife</u>: Add flour, sugar, salt, butter and shortening to bowl -- about 5 quick on/off turns until mixture resembles coarse meal. With machine running, pour ice water through feed tube -- stop machine once dough is in a ball. Remove dough, flatten, wrap in plastic, refrigerate for at least 2 hours. Pastry can be frozen, wrapped airtight.

<u>Apple Mixture</u>. Peel apples, drop in water with lemon juice or vitamin C tablet. In a 10-inch round metal cake pan at least 1-1/4 inches deep,

(continued on other side)

LA TARTE TATIN (cont.)

place sugar and water. Set over high heat until mixture has a caramel color, shaking pan occasionally. Quarter, core apples.

<u>Serrated Slicer</u>: Stack apple quarters horizontally in feed tube, 2 at a time, and slice. Arrange slightly overlapping apple slices, rounded side down, starting around outside edge of pan with the slices pointing towards the center. Fill in center with more overlapping circles of apple slices. Sprinkle with cinnamon and lemon zest. Dot with butter. Bake in preheated 400 degree oven for 30 minutes.

Roll out pastry dough to slightly larger circle than pan; lay over pan, cut off excess dough with rolling pin. Cut 3 slashes in crust to release steam. Continue to bake in 425 degree oven for 20 minutes. Allow tarte to cool in pan for 10 minutes, then invert onto a serving platter. Heat preserves, Cognac and water until proper consistency to spread -- sieve, then brush glaze on tart while it is still hot.

<u>Sauce</u>. <u>Plastic Knife</u>: Combine sour cream with 3 to 4 tablespoons Greek vanilla syrup. Serve tarte warm with sauce.

*Available at specialty food stores. As a substitution for Greek vanilla syrup, use 3 tablespoons confectioners sugar mixed with 1/2 teaspoon vanilla and 1 inch vanilla bean, split and scraped.

Makes 8 servings.

FRENCH BREAD

Foolproof, fast and about as good as any you will find outside of Paris.

2-1/2 cups unbleached all-purpose flour
  1/2 cup cake flour
    1 teaspoon salt
  1/2 package active dry yeast (1 teaspoon)
    1 cup warm water (105 to 115 degrees)

Glaze

    1 egg beaten
  1/2 teaspoon salt

Combine flours and salt. Dissolve yeast in warm water. <u>Steel Knife</u>: Add 2 cups flour with 1/2 dissolved yeast mixture -- 4 quick on/off turns. Add balance of liquid, repeating on/off motion. Add 3/4 cup remaining flour, repeat on/off motion 4 times, then let machine run until dough forms a ball. Stop machine, touch dough. If too wet and sticky, add remaining flour. Turn on machine to knead dough until smooth, but still sticky to the touch.

Place in lightly oiled bowl, turning dough so entire surface is oiled. Cover with damp towel and let rise in warm place (about 80 degrees) until doubled in bulk, 1 to 2 hours.

Remove to lightly floured board, roll out to desired length, roll up tightly starting with long side. Stretch end pieces so seams are under loaf. Pinch seams together. Place on baking sheet sprinkled with cornmeal. Slash top with <u>Steel Knife</u> from food processor. Cover with damp towel and let rise again until doubled.

<u>Plastic Knife</u>: Mix egg and salt for glaze -- 6 on/off turns. Brush on glaze very carefully without dripping onto baking sheet. Bake in preheated 400 degree oven 30 minutes or until loaf is browned and sounds hollow when tapped on bottom. For extra crispness, brush crust lightly with water when bread is removed from oven.

Makes 1 loaf.

NOTES

A FISH DINNER

Green Onion Quiche

* * *

Stuffed Fish en Papillote

Carrot and Turnip Purée

Matchstick Potatoes

* * *

Cauliflower, Radish, Green Pepper Slaw

Tarragon Vinaigrette

* * *

Lemon Cream Puffs

with

Lemon Curd

GREEN ONION QUICHE

A variation of the traditional quiche. It is an excellent hors d'oeuvre or luncheon dish.

Pâte Brisée

1-1/2 cups unbleached all-purpose flour
  1/2 teaspoon salt
    1 egg yolk
    4 ounces (1 stick) chilled unsalted butter,
      cut in 6 pieces
    5 tablespoons ice water

Filling

   12 scallions, cut in thirds
    3 tablespoons butter
    1 tablespoon oil
    1 tablespoon flour
    6 ounces Swiss cheese (1-1/2 cups shredded)
    4 USDA large eggs
1-1/3 cups half and half
    1 teaspoon salt
      Freshly ground black pepper
    1 teaspoon oregano

Pâte Brisée. Steel Knife: Place flour, salt, egg yolk and butter in bowl. Turn machine on/off until mixture resembles coarse meal. With machine running, pour ice water through feed tube -- stop machine once dough is in a ball. Remove dough, press flat, wrap in plastic and chill at least 2 hours. Roll out on lightly floured board, place in buttered 11-inch quiche pan, prick bottom and sides with a fork, refrigerate 30 minutes or until firm. Line with parchment paper, fill with beans or rice, bake in pre-heated 400 degree oven 12 minutes. Remove paper and beans, prick crust again, bake 6 minutes longer or until crust is lightly browned. This will produce a crisp crust that resists moisture.

Filling. Serrated Slicer: Slice scallions, wedged vertically in feed tube. Melt butter and heat oil. Mix in scallions, blend in flour and simply warm through. Shredder: Shred cheese, set aside. Plastic Knife: Lightly beat eggs -- 4 quick on/off turns. Add half and half -- 2 quick on/off turns. Pour into mixing bowl, add salt, pepper, scallions and cheese; mix well. Pour into prepared pie shell, being careful not to fill crust to the very top -- within 1/8 inch of top edge. Sprinkle with oregano. Bake in pre-heated 375 degree oven 30 to 40 minutes or until well colored. Let rest 10 minutes before serving -- can also be served at room temperature.

Makes 6 to 8 servings.

STUFFED FISH EN PAPILLOTE

The mushroom stuffing may be used as an appetizer spread, too.

Stuffing

3/4 cup parsley leaves, firmly packed
 1 small onion, peeled, quartered (1/4 cup minced)
 1 tablespoon butter
 2 tablespoons water
 1 pound mushrooms (2 cups minced)
 1 teaspoon dried dill weed
 1 teaspoon salt
   Freshly ground black pepper

Fish

   1 6-pound whitefish or trout or
   2 3-pound sea bass or
   8 rainbow trout
     Salt
     Freshly ground black pepper
1/8 cup fresh lemon juice
   1 small firm tomato (1/2 cup sliced)
   1 small lemon, scored
   1 small onion, peeled (1/2 cup sliced)
   4 tablespoons butter
     Dried dill weed
     Seaweed (optional)
1/2 cup dry white wine or dry vermouth

Stuffing. Steel Knife: Mince parsley -- quick on/off turns. Set aside, reserving 1/4 cup for final garnish. Mince onion -- quick on/off turns. Cook onion in butter and water until water has evaporated. Mince mushrooms in 2 batches -- quick on/off turns. Add to onion, cook 5 minutes. Remove from heat, add 1/2 cup minced parsley, dill weed, salt, pepper. Adjust seasoning -- must be generous because of subtle flavor of fish.

Fish. Keep fish head and tail intact, have fish boned and prepared for stuffing. Wash fish in cold water, dry with paper towels. Sprinkle fish inside and out with lemon juice. Season cavity of fish lightly with salt and pepper. Lay fish on large piece of buttered foil, spoon stuffing inside (do not overstuff), skewer together. Serrated Slicer: Slice tomato, using gentle pressure. Slice lemon (cut flat ends), using firm pressure. Slice onion, using medium pressure. Alternate tomato and lemon slices on fish. Top with onion rings. Dot surface with butter, lightly season with salt, pepper and dill weed. Surround with ring of seaweed, pour wine around fish. Close foil so it forms a loose fitting airtight package. Bake in preheated 350 degree oven for 40 minutes, open packet to check fish. Cook longer if necessary. Arrange on a platter, sprinkle with reserved 1/4 cup minced parsley, surround with lemon wedges, parsley sprigs.

Makes 8 servings.

CARROT AND TURNIP PUREE

This blend of vegetables has a surprising and most pleasant flavor.

```
  2 pounds carrots, peeled, cut in 2-inch lengths
  2 turnips (6 ounces), peeled, quartered
1/4 cup parsley leaves, firmly packed
  3 tablespoons butter
  1 teaspoon freshly grated nutmeg
    Salt
    Freshly ground black pepper
```

Use steamer or pressure cooker to cook carrots. Cook turnips in salted water to cover until very tender. Drain.

Steel Knife: Mince parsley -- quick on/off turns. Set aside for garnish. Process carrots and turnips in 1-1/2 cup batches -- 2 quick on/off turns, then let machine run until vegetables are puréed, about 10 seconds. Place in bowl, mix well together, add butter, season to taste. Place in buttered casserole. This can be prepared in advance.

Place casserole in pan of water (bain-marie), bring to boil on top of the stove, bake in 350 degree oven for 40 minutes, covered with buttered parchment paper. Sprinkle with minced parsley before serving.

Makes 6 to 8 servings.

MATCHSTICK POTATOES

Here's real one-upmanship with the Cuisinart® food processor. After you slice the potatoes twice, as specified in the recipe, you end up with uniformly matched potato sticks.

6 large potatoes, peeled
  Oil to cover bottom of pan

Trim potatoes to largest size that will fit feed tube. <u>Serrated Slicer</u>: Slice potatoes, remove slices from bowl. Hold cover upside down, insert pusher so as to leave a cup an inch deep at bottom of feed tube. Stack potato slices vertically in this cup, making sure to wedge last slice in so potatoes will not fall out when cover is placed back on bowl. Slice, using medium pressure, forming a julienne cut. Repeat until all potatoes are processed.

Soak cut potatoes in ice water to remove starch, dry with paper towels. Sauté in well heated oil in batches. Brown well on one side, then turn with metal spatula and brown on other side. Keep cooked potatoes warm in oven until all potatoes are cooked.

Makes 8 servings.

CAULIFLOWER, RADISH, GREEN PEPPER SLAW

An interesting variation of an old standby.

Salad

1/2 cup parsley or watercress leaves, firmly packed
  2 shallots, peeled (1/8 cup minced)
  1 small head cabbage, cut in wedges to fit feed tube, (4 cups sliced)
  6 ounces cauliflower, divided into flowerets, (2 cups sliced)
  2 cups radishes (2 cups sliced)
  1 stalk celery (1 cup sliced)
  1 small green pepper, seeded (1 cup sliced)

Tarragon Vinaigrette

1/2 cup oil
  1 tablespoon lemon juice
  5 tablespoons tarragon vinegar
  1 teaspoon thyme
  1 teaspoon tarragon
  1 teaspoon basil
  1 teaspoon celery seed
  2 teaspoons sugar
  1 teaspoon salt
    Freshly ground black pepper

As each vegetable is processed, place in salad bowl. Steel Knife: Mince parsley or watercress -- quick on/off turns. Mince shallots -- drop through feed tube with machine running. Serrated Slicer: Slice cabbage. (Use Steel Knife to chop any coarse or irregular pieces -- quick on/off turns). Slice cauliflowerets, radishes, celery and green pepper. Reserve green pepper slices for garnish.

Plastic Knife: Mix vinaigrette ingredients. Add more oil to taste. Combine with salad, adjust seasoning, garnish with green pepper slices, chill thoroughly.

Makes 8 servings.

LEMON CREAM PUFFS

An always popular dessert -- and prepared so much faster than the classical way.

Glaze

  1 egg
1/2 teaspoon salt

Pâte à Choux

2/3 cup water
1/3 stick unsalted butter
1/4 teaspoon salt
  1 teaspoon sugar
2/3 cup flour
  3 USDA large eggs

Filling

1/2 cup whipping cream
1/2 cup Lemon Curd (see basic recipes)*
1/3 cup Crème Fraîche (see basic recipes)*
    Zest of 1 lemon
  1 tablespoon lemon juice
1/2 teaspoon lemon flavoring

Glaze. Plastic Knife: Mix egg with salt -- 6 quick on/off turns. Set aside. Covered and refrigerated will last one week.

Pâte à Choux. Preheat oven to 400 degrees. Bring water slowly to boil with butter, salt, sugar. When butter is melted, stir in the flour vigorously until all the flour is absorbed. Steel Knife: Spoon flour mixture into machine bowl. Add eggs. Mix well by letting machine run 20 seconds. The mixture should be thick and hold its shape when lifted on a spoon.

Butter 2 baking sheets and dampen with water. Put dough into pastry bag fitted with 1/4-inch or 1/2-inch plain tube and pipe 1-inch or 2-inch mounds of dough onto sheets. Brush puffs with glaze. Be sure to prevent any excess glaze from dripping onto pan and brush down little peaks of dough which would burn easily. Bake in preheated 400 degree oven for 10 minutes, then raise oven temperature to 425 degrees and bake for 20 minutes or until puffs are firm and brown. Let cool completely, cut off tops and remove any softened dough inside puffs.

Filling. Whip cream with mixer until stiff. Beat in Lemon Curd, Crème Fraîche, lemon zest, lemon juice and lemon flavoring. Fill cooled pâte à choux with lemon cream mixture.

*Also available at specialty food stores.

Makes 24 small or 12 large cream puffs.

NOTES

A GREEK DINNER

Spinach-Feta Strudel

or

Taramosalada

* * *

Lemon Shish Kebabs

Moussaka

* * *

Greek Salad

* * *

Wheat Germ Bread

* * *

Sliced Oranges Grand Marnier

Strawberry Sauce

SPINACH-FETA STRUDEL

Tempting as an appetizer, a luncheon or supper main course, or as a vegetable dish for a buffet.

```
  1 package frozen strudel leaves
  2 pounds fresh spinach
  1 thin slice bread (1/2 cup bread crumbs)
2/3 cup parsley leaves, firmly packed (1/3 cup minced)
 12 scallions (1/2 cup minced)
  4 tablespoons butter
  6 ounces feta cheese, chilled (1-1/2 cups sliced)
  4 tablespoons fresh dill or
  2 tablespoons dried dill weed
  4 USDA large eggs
    Salt
    Freshly ground black pepper
  4 ounces (1 stick) melted butter
```

Thaw strudel leaves by removing from refrigerator 4 hours before using. Wash spinach, cut off root ends only -- leave stems. With only water clinging to leaves, cook quickly in uncovered pot. As soon as spinach wilts, refresh in cold water, drain, pat dry with paper towels.

Steel Knife: Chop bread, torn into pieces -- let machine run until crumbs are desired size. Set aside. Mince parsley -- quick on/off turns, set aside. Mince scallions -- quick on/off turns (these will later be puréed with spinach), sauté in 4 tablespoons butter until soft. Serrated Slicer: Slice chilled cheese, then insert Steel Knife: Chop with fresh dill -- 3 quick on/off turns. Place in a mixing bowl. Purée spinach, scallions and eggs -- let machine run until well mixed. Add to cheese mixture, mix in parsley, seasonings. Taste for seasoning -- should be over seasoned to the taste.

Butter a baking sheet. Place a strudel leaf on a damp towel (cover remaining leaves with damp cloth to prevent drying out). Brush leaf with melted butter, sprinkle lightly with bread crumbs. Repeat 3 more times as 3 more strudel leaves are added in layers. Place 1/3 of spinach mixture 1/4 inch from edge along longer side of dough which should be placed nearest you. Roll like a jelly roll with the assistance of a towel. Place on baking sheet. Brush top lightly with melted butter.

This recipe makes 3 strudel rolls; repeat 2 more times. Bake in preheated 375 degree oven 30 to 35 minutes or until browned. Unused strudel leaves can be refrozen.

Makes 10 servings.

TARAMOSALADA

A delicious adaptation of a favorite ethnic spread. It will last a week, covered and refrigerated.

    1/4 cup parsley leaves, firmly packed (1/8 cup minced)
      1 small onion, peeled and quartered (1/4 cup minced)
      2 large potatoes (3/4 pound total), cooked, cooled,
        peeled and quartered
    1/2 cup (4 ounces) tarama*
      3 tablespoons fresh lemon juice
      1 cup oil (I use safflower -- use oil of your choice)

<u>Steel Knife</u>: Mince parsley -- on/off turns, set aside. Mince onion -- on/off turns. Add potatoes, tarama, lemon juice. Turn machine on/off 4 times to blend. With machine running, pour oil in steady stream through feed tube until mixture is thickened. Spoon into a crock. Garnish with minced parsley; cover and refrigerate. Serve on thin slices of French bread, cucumber slices or crackers.

*Tarama is red carp roe from Greece, available at specialty food markets.

Makes about 3 cups.

LEMON SHISH KEBABS

With the lemons sliced as only the Cuisinart® food processor can do them, this lamb kebab is an aesthetic delight.

Marinade

    1/2 cup parsley leaves, firmly packed (1/4 cup minced)
      2 cloves garlic
      1 medium onion, peeled and quartered
      1 cup oil
    1/3 cup fresh lemon juice
      2 tablespoons Cavender's Greek Seasoning*
1-1/2 teaspoons salt
        Freshly ground black pepper

      4 pounds beef (sirloin tip) or lamb (from the leg)
    32 mushroom caps
      3 lemons, ends cut off, scored
        Red or green pepper, cut in squares
        Cherry tomatoes
        Parsley

Steel Knife: Mince parsley -- quick on/off turns. Set aside. With machine running, add garlic through feed tube. Mince onion -- quick on/off turns. Add oil, lemon juice, seasonings -- quick on/off turns to combine ingredients. Place in large bowl.

Cut meat into 32 pieces; add to marinade and stir to coat evenly. Cover and refrigerate overnight. A few hours before cooking, add mushrooms to marinade.

Serrated Slicer: Insert lemons from base of feed tube, if slightly too large for top of feed tube. Apply firm, not hard, pressure to slice. Place meat on skewers, alternating with lemon slices, pepper squares, mushroom caps. Brush with marinade; broil on charcoal or in broiler, 4 inches from heat -- turn and baste again. Watch carefully if meat is desired rare. Garnish platter with cherry tomatoes and parsley.

*This blend of salt, pepper, garlic, oregano, beef flavor and seven other spices is available at specialty food stores. As a substitute for it, mix together 4 teaspoons salt, 1 teaspoon mashed bouillon cubes or granulated bouillon, 1/2 teaspoon ground black pepper, 1/2 teaspoon oregano, 1/8 teaspoon garlic powder and, as an optional ingredient, 1/4 teaspoon monosodium glutamate.

Makes 8 servings.

MOUSSAKA

This eggplant dish holds its shape when served either hot or at room temperature.

       3 medium (2-1/4 pounds total) eggplants
         (about 10 cups sliced)
       2 tablespoons salt
       3 ounces Parmesan cheese, at room
         temperature (3/4 cup shredded)
     1/2 cup parsley leaves, firmly packed
         (1/4 cup minced)
   1-1/2 large onions, peeled and quartered
         (1-1/2 cup minced)
       6 tablespoons oil
       4 tablespoons tomato paste
     1/3 cup dry white or red wine
     3/4 teaspoon cinnamon
       1 teaspoon salt
         Freshly ground black pepper

Topping

       4 tablespoons butter
       3 tablespoons flour
       2 cups milk
       1 teaspoon salt
         Freshly ground white pepper
       2 USDA large eggs
     1/2 teaspoon freshly ground nutmeg
   1-1/4 cups ricotta or cottage cheese

Cut unpeeled eggplant into largest size wedges to fit into feed tube. <u>Serrated Slicer</u>: Slice, using medium pressure. Place in colander, mix with 2 tablespoons salt. Allow to drain for 30 minutes. <u>Shredder</u>: Shred cheese, using light pressure (be sure cheese can be cut with a knife); set aside. <u>Steel Knife</u>: Mince parsley -- quick on/off turns. Set aside. Mince onions -- quick on/off turns.

Sauté onions in 2 tablespoons oil, covered, until soft. Add parsley, tomato paste, wine, cinnamon, salt, pepper -- adjust seasonings. Set aside. Drain eggplant, rinse with cold water; pat very dry with paper towels. Sauté in 4 tablespoons oil, covered, shaking pan to stir eggplant -- just steam through, do not overcook.

Butter a 13-inch round ovenproof dish -- add the eggplant in layers, season lightly with salt, pepper. Sprinkle with 1/4 cup Parmesan cheese. Spread tomato mixture over eggplant. Sprinkle with 1/2 cup Parmesan cheese.

(continued on other side)

MOUSSAKA (cont.)

<u>Topping</u>. In a saucepan, melt butter and make a roux with flour, blending well -- cook together 5 minutes. Add milk, stirring constantly. Cook until mixture is smooth and thickened. Season with 1 teaspoon salt and pepper to taste. Remove from heat, cool slightly. <u>Plastic Knife</u>: Blend eggs, nutmeg, ricotta cheese -- quick on/off turns. Mix into cream sauce -- adjust seasoning. Pour sauce over top of casserole. Bake in pre-heated 375 degree oven for 1 hour or until golden. Let cool 20 to 30 minutes before serving.

<u>Variation</u>. Two cups minced leftover lamb or beef can be added to the tomato mixture. Increase tomato paste to 6 tablespoons and wine to 2/3 cup. Adjust seasoning.

Makes 8 servings.

GREEK SALAD

What makes this an all-time favorite is the combination of olives, red onion and feta cheese.

Dressing

3/4 cup oil
1/4 cup red wine vinegar
1/8 teaspoon dry mustard
2 teaspoons Cavender's Greek Seasoning*
1 teaspoon salt
Freshly ground black pepper
1 teaspoon oregano
2 tablespoons fresh dill or
1 teaspoon dried dill weed

Salad

3 medium heads romaine lettuce
1/2 cup parsley leaves, firmly packed (1/4 cup minced)
2 green peppers, seeded
10 radishes
2 pickled cucumbers or
1 fresh cucumber
1 small red onion (1/3 cup sliced)
6 ounces feta cheese, chilled (1-1/2 cups sliced)
16 cherry tomatoes
16 Calamata olives, drained
8 anchovy fillets (optional)

Dressing. Plastic Knife: Place all ingredients in bowl -- 2 quick on/off turns. Do not over salt -- feta cheese contains salt.

Salad. Wash, dry and tear romaine into bite-size pieces. Steel Knife: Mince parsley -- quick on/off turns; set aside for garnish. Serrated Slicer: Slice green peppers (if too large to fit top of feed tube, try to insert from the bottom -- or cut green pepper lengthwise on one side and roll it into a tight coil), radishes, cucumber, red onion. Remove vegetables to salad bowl. Slice feta, then insert Steel Knife -- 2 quick on/off turns to chop coarsely. Combine salad ingredients, mix in dressing, adjust seasonings. garnish with minced parsley.

*This blend of salt, pepper, garlic, oregano, beef flavor and seven other spices is available at specialty food stores.

Makes 8 servings.

WHEAT GERM BREAD

This loaf has great texture. If you prefer even more, add another 1/4 cup wheat germ and use only 1-3/4 cups unbleached flour.

Glaze

  1 egg
1/2 teaspoon salt

  1 cup warm water (105 to 115 degrees)
  1 package active dry yeast
  1 teaspoon sugar
  2 cups unbleached all-purpose flour
3/4 cup cake flour
1/4 cup wheat germ
  1 teaspoon salt
    Additional wheat germ or sesame seed

Plastic Knife: Mix egg and salt -- 4 quick on/off turns. Set aside, covered and refrigerated.

Mix warm water, yeast, sugar; proof. Mix flours, wheat germ and salt together. Steel Knife: Place 2/3 of flour mixture into bowl, add 1/2 of yeast mixture; turn machine on/off to incorporate. Repeat with remaining yeast. Add all but 1/2 cup flour, turn machine on/off, then let run until dough forms a ball. Stop machine and touch -- if dough is too sticky, add a little flour. Repeat this. When dough is of proper consistency, let machine run to knead dough (no more than 60 seconds). When smooth, remove to oiled bowl -- turn dough so oiled all over. Cover with damp cloth and let rise in warm place (80 degrees) until doubled in quantity.

Roll out to rectangular shape on floured board, form into a loaf, pinch seam to seal and pull ends down under loaf. Place seam side down in an oiled 10-inch bread pan. Slash with steel knife. Cover with damp cloth; let rise until doubled again. Brush with glaze -- sprinkle top with wheat germ or sesame seeds. Bake in a preheated 400 degree oven for 30 minutes or until browned and a hollow sound results from tapping bottom of loaf.

Makes a 10-inch loaf.

SLICED ORANGES GRAND MARNIER, STRAWBERRY SAUCE

If you want to gild the lily, serve this dessert with pastries from your favorite Greek bakery.

```
    Zest of 2 oranges
  8 navel oranges (not over 2-1/2 inches diameter), peeled
  2 tablespoons sugar
  4 tablespoons Grand Marnier
```

Strawberry Sauce

```
    2 pints strawberries
    4 tablespoons sugar
1/2 cup currant jelly, melted
    2 tablespoons Grand Marnier
    2 tablespoons imported Kirsch
    1 teaspoon fresh lemon juice
```

Remove zest from 2 oranges with vegetable peeler. Cut flat ends on oranges. Place each on cutting board and cut off peel with a sharp knife, leaving no white membranes.

Steel Knife: Mince zest with 2 tablespoons sugar -- let machine run until desired fineness. Serrated Slicer: Shape orange so it will fit into feed tube; do not cut in half. (Remember to try inserting it through bottom of feed tube.) Slice. Chill sliced oranges in mixture of 4 tablespoons Grand Marnier, zest and sugar.

Steel Knife: Purée 1-1/2 pints strawberries (save largest for slicing) with 2 tablespoons sugar. Add melted jelly, 2 tablespoons Grand Marnier, Kirsch, lemon juice and 2 tablespoons sugar -- quick on/off turns until blended. Serrated Slicer: Slice remaining strawberries using light pressure. Fold gently into sauce. Refrigerate. Serve on the side.

Makes 8 servings.

NOTES

PICNIC FARE

French Country Pâté

Eggs Cressonière

* * *

Broiled Tarragon Chicken Breasts

* * *

Sliced Tomatoes, Basil Vinaigrette

* * *

Caper Mayonnaise Salad

Cheese Bread

* * *

Chocolate Torte

FRENCH COUNTRY PATE

Without a Cuisinart® food processor, it would take hours to make this pâté. You can do it in much less than one hour. For best flavor, refrigerate three to five days before serving.

```
      6 slices bacon
    1/4 cup pistachio nuts
    1/4 pound chicken livers
      4 tablespoons butter
    1/2 cup parsley leaves, firmly packed (1/4 cup minced)
    1/2 slice bread (1/4 cup bread crumbs)
      2 garlic cloves, peeled
      1 medium onion, peeled and quartered (1 cup minced)
  1-1/2 pounds boneless pork (loin preferred), cut in 1-inch pieces
  1-1/2 pounds boneless veal (not shank or stewing meat), cut in 1-inch pieces
    1/2 pound smoked ham, cut in 1-inch pieces
      3 USDA large eggs
    1/2 cup Cognac
      2 teaspoons salt, or to taste
      1 teaspoon mixed herbs, combining savory, thyme and oregano
    1/2 teaspoon allspice
    1/2 teaspoon cinnamon
    1/2 teaspoon freshly grated nutmeg
```

Blanch bacon -- place bacon slices in cold water to cover, let simmer 5 minutes, remove to paper towels, pat dry. Skin pistachios -- drop into boiling water 1 minute, rub skins off with towel. Sauté chicken livers in 2 tablespoons butter.

Steel Knife: Mince parsley and bread -- quick on/off turns. Remove and set aside. Mince garlic -- with machine running, drop cloves through feed tube to mince finely. Mince onions -- quick on/off turns. Sauté onion and garlic until soft in 2 tablespoons butter. Chop pork and veal in small batches -- 6 pieces at a time -- quick on/off turns. Chop ham coarsely -- quick on/off turns. Purée sautéed chicken livers with 3 bacon slices. Mix all ingredients together reserving 3 bacon slices. Sauté a sample to taste for seasoning; adjust seasoning if necessary.

Butter a 6-cup terrine or loaf pan -- line bottom with parchment paper. Spoon in pâté mixture, banging pan down to eliminate air bubbles. Top with reserved bacon slices. Cover with terrine lid or foil. Place in bain-marie or water bath with water coming 1/2 way up terrine. Bring to boil on top of stove, then bake in preheated 350 degree oven for 2-1/2 hours. As pâté cools, weight it down (bricks wrapped in foil work well). Chill thoroughly before serving. This freezes very well. Serve in thin slices with French cornichons (tiny pickles with a sour, spicy flavor) and a variety of mustards -- lemon and green peppercorn French mustards are especially good.

Makes 12 servings.

EGGS CRESSONIERE

These are an easy version of deviled eggs -- perfect for picnics or as an appetizer.

```
  2 shallots, peeled
1/2 cup mayonnaise
1/2 bunch watercress, blanched
1/4 cup parsley leaves, firmly packed (1/8 cup minced)
1/2 teaspoon dried basil
  1 teaspoon dried dill
1/8 teaspoon curry powder
1/8 teaspoon cayenne pepper
1/2 teaspoon Dijon mustard
    Salt
    Freshly ground black pepper
  8 hard-cooked eggs, peeled, quartered
    Lettuce
    Watercress sprigs
```

<u>Steel Knife</u>: Mince shallots -- quick on/off turns. Add all other ingredients except eggs, lettuce and watercress -- turn machine on/off until sauce is smooth and uniform, about 10 seconds. Taste and adjust seasonings.

Arrange eggs on a lettuce-lined platter. Cover each quarter with a dollop of sauce. Garnish with watercress sprigs. Sauce can be served separately on the side.

Makes 8 servings.

BROILED TARRAGON CHICKEN BREASTS

The tantalizing flavor of herb butter inserted under the skin of chicken breasts is a tasty surprise.

```
      1 shallot, peeled
      1 clove garlic, peeled
    1/2 cup parsley leaves, firmly packed (1/4 cup minced)
  1-1/2 sticks unsalted butter, cut in pieces
      2 teaspoons dried tarragon
  1-1/2 teaspoons salt
        Freshly ground black pepper
      6 chicken breasts, split in half
```

Steel Knife: Mince shallot, garlic, parsley together -- quick on/off turns. Add remaining ingredients except chicken breasts -- quick on/off turns until combined, then let machine run until mixture is puréed.

Loosen skin on each breast with fingers making a pocket without tearing the skin. Place 1 tablespoon of herb mixture in pocket of each. Spread by pressing outside of chicken.

Place chicken skin side down on rack in broiling pan about 7 to 9 inches from source of heat (or at 450 degrees). Season other side with salt and pepper to taste. Broil until browned, about 15 minutes. Turn chicken, season skin lightly with salt and pepper; broil 20 minutes longer or until browned and tender. Cool to room temperature. Chicken breasts can be prepared, ready to cook, a day in advance, covered and refrigerated.

Makes 12 servings.

SLICED TOMATOES, BASIL VINAIGRETTE

- 1/2 cup parsley leaves, firmly packed (1/4 cup minced)
- 3 teaspoons fresh basil leaves or
- 1-1/2 teaspoons dried basil
- 1 shallot, peeled
- 3/4 cup oil
- 1/4 cup red wine vinegar
- 1/2 teaspoon salt
- Freshly ground black pepper
- 14 Italian, 8 small or 6 medium tomatoes, all slightly underripe

Steel Knife: Mince parsley, basil and shallot together -- quick on/off turns. Empty contents into mixing bowl -- combine with oil, vinegar, salt and pepper to taste.

Serrated Slicer: Cut flat ends on tomatoes, cut in half if necessary to fit into feed tube -- with light pressure on pusher, slice. Place slices in dish, pour over vinaigrette, adjust seasoning. The tomatoes can be served immediately or they can marinate several hours.

Makes 8 servings.

CAPER MAYONNAISE SALAD

A fresh and refreshing combination to "sandwich" in bread or to serve on a bed of lettuce leaves.

1/2 cup parsley leaves, firmly packed (1/4 cup minced)
1 medium red onion, peeled and quartered (1/2 cup minced)
1/2 cucumber, unpeeled, cut in half lengthwise, seeded
    cut in half again (1 cup chopped)
1 small red pepper, seeded (3/4 cup sliced)
1 small green pepper, seeded (3/4 cup sliced)
12 pitted black olives
1/4 cup capers, drained
3/4 cup mayonnaise
1 teaspoon anchovy paste
  Salt
  Freshly ground black pepper

As each ingredient (except parsley) is processed, place into sieve to allow liquid to drain off. <u>Steel Knife</u>: Mince parsley -- quick on/off turns, set aside. Mince onion -- quick on/off turns. Coarsely chop cucumber -- quick on/off turns, checking carefully -- do not mince too small. <u>Serrated Slicer</u>: Slice peppers (substitute 1/3 cup pimiento, julienned with a knife, if red pepper is not available). Olives -- cut flat ends -- start mounding them on blade, then set cover on and finish filling feed tube from the top. Slice, using light pressure. <u>Steel Knife</u>: Purée capers (rinsed, patted dry in paper towels) with mayonnaise and anchovy paste -- on/off turns.

Combine drained vegetables and parsley with mayonnaise mixture. Season to taste with salt and pepper. This salad can be prepared a day in advance.

To serve as a filling for bread, cut a loaf of Cheese Bread (recipe follows) or French bread horizontally 1/3 from the top, leaving one side intact. Some of the bread from the larger bottom piece can be pulled out so there is space for more filling. Fill bread with salad mixture -- do not overfill. This can be done 2 hours in advance, then wrapped in foil. If assembled in advance, Cheese Bread is preferable to French bread since its crisp crust resists sogginess. Slice through when ready to serve.

When serving as a salad, save minced parsley for garnish on top of salad mixture. Serve on lettuce leaves surrounded with tomato wedges.

Makes about 3 cups.

CHEESE BREAD

This is the bread my students voted "the best". Perhaps the crustiness accounts for its popularity -- or that special tang of the Swiss cheese. For a milder cheese flavor, substitute mozzarella for the Swiss.

- 1-1/2 ounces Swiss cheese (1/2 cup shredded)
- 1 package active dry yeast
- 1 teaspoon sugar
- 1 cup warm water (105 to 115 degrees)
- 2 cups unbleached all-purpose flour
- 1/2 cup cake flour
- 1 teaspoon salt

Glaze

- 1 egg
- 1/2 teaspoon salt

- 1 tablespoon oil
- 2 tablespoons cornmeal

Shredder: Shred cheese, set aside. Proof yeast -- mix yeast, sugar and water together. Let stand about 10 minutes until foam rises to top. Combine flours and salt.

Plastic Knife: Mix egg and salt for glaze -- 4 quick on/off turns. Set aside, covered and refrigerated.

Steel Knife: Place 2 cups flour mixture in bowl, add 1/2 the liquid mixture, turn machine on/off 4 times. Add balance of liquid, 3/4 of remaining flour, shredded cheese -- repeat 4 on/off turns, then let machine run until dough forms a ball. Stop machine, touch dough. If too sticky (wet), add remaining flour by tablespoons, stopping machine after each addition to touch dough. The dough should be slightly sticky. When it is the correct consistency, turn machine on to knead dough until smooth (about 40 to 60 seconds), but still sticky to the touch.

Place in a lightly oiled ceramic bowl, turning dough so oiled all over. Cover with damp towel, place where temperature is 75 to 80 degrees, leave until doubled in bulk, about 1 hour. Remove to lightly floured board. Roll out to a rectangle, form loaf by rolling tightly, pinching out air bubbles. Make tight seam, press ends and tuck under loaf; place seam side down on bread pan (French or Italian shape) brushed with oil and sprinkled with cornmeal. Slash top of loaf with Steel Knife from food processor, cover with damp towel and let rise again until doubled, about 1 hour.

(continued on other side)

CHEESE BREAD (cont.)

Brush loaf with glaze and bake in preheated 400 degree oven 30 minutes or until loaf is brown and sounds hollow when tapped on the bottom. For extra crispness, brush lightly with water immediately after bread is removed from oven.

Makes 1 long loaf.

CHOCOLATE TORTE

One of my very best recipes. Unlike some chocolate tortes, this one can be cut into perfect thin slices.

```
1/4 slice bread (5 tablespoons crumbs)
  2 cups almonds, walnuts or pecans (2 cups ground)
  6 ounces sweet chocolate, preferably Maillard's, then German
  1 tablespoon baking powder
1/2 cup (1 stick) unsalted butter, cut in pieces
  1 cup sugar
  7 USDA large eggs, separated
  2 teaspoons rum
    Pinch salt
```

Glaze

```
    3 ounces sweet chocolate
    2 tablespoons water
    2 tablespoons butter
    4 tablespoons sifted confectioners sugar
    1 tablespoon rum
```

Butter an 8-inch springform pan. Line bottom with parchment paper. Place following ingredients in large mixing bowl as processed. Steel Knife: Make bread crumbs -- quick on/off turns. Finely chop nuts -- quick on/off turns, let machine run 10 seconds, check texture -- can be coarse or fine (set aside 2 tablespoons to garnish cake). Chop chocolate -- on/off turns. Let machine run 10 seconds, check texture -- some coarse pieces the size of a pea create a delicious taste.

Mix processed ingredients with baking powder. Steel Knife: Cream butter and sugar, letting machine run until mixture forms a ball. Add egg yolks, rum and salt -- quick on/off turns only until yolks are absorbed. Combine with chocolate mixture -- mix together thoroughly.

With electric mixer, beat egg whites until stiff (not dry), then gently fold into mixture. Pour into prepared springform pan and bake in preheated 350 degree oven for 60 minutes. Let cool in pan on wire rack. To remove, carefully wedge knife around sides, separating cake from pan. This cake improves with refrigeration and freezes well unglazed.

Glaze. Mix all ingredients (except rum) in top of double boiler. Cook slowly until heated. Add rum. Spread on cake; sprinkle reserved nuts on top and sides.

Makes 12 servings.

NOTES

AN ORIENTAL MEAL

Chinese Lettuce Appetizers

* * *

Beef with Broccoli, Water Chestnuts and Mushrooms

Chinese Noodles Supreme

* * *

Japanese Relish

* * *

Apricot Mousse in Orange Shells

Sablés

BEEF WITH BROCCOLI, WATER CHESTNUTS & MUSHROOMS

The outstanding feature of this dish is the contrast of textures between meat and vegetables. The key to its success is the precooking of the broccoli. Please note this carefully, it's essential.

Marinade

```
     3 tablespoons dry sherry
 1-1/2 teaspoons sugar
   1/2 cup oyster sauce*
     3 tablespoons light soy sauce*

     2 garlic cloves, peeled
     2 pounds beef bottom round roast, cut in pieces to fit
       feed tube, then frozen
 1-1/2 pounds broccoli (3 cups stem slices and flowerets)
    10 water chestnuts, drained
     8 large mushrooms
   1/2 cup peanut oil
   1/2 teaspoon salt
     1 slice (1 inch) fresh ginger, peeled
```

Place marinade ingredients in a 11-1/2 x 13-inch (gallon size) plastic bag, twist tie, shake to combine.

Steel Knife: Mince garlic (with machine running, drop garlic through feed tube). Remove and set aside. Serrated Slicer: Slice beef (remove from freezer 15 minutes before slicing -- defrost only until the point of a knife can be inserted in the meat). Add meat to bag containing marinade and marinate at least 30 minutes, turning over a few times.

Peel stems of broccoli, divide. Cut off flowerets, divide. Serrated Slicer: Slice stems. Drop all broccoli pieces into boiling salted water for 2 minutes; drain, refresh immediately in cold water; drain and pat dry with paper towels. Slice water chestnuts and mushrooms.

Heat 2 tablespoons oil in wok or skillet. Add sliced broccoli stems, salt; stir-fry 1 minute. Add flowerets, stir-fry 1 minute more. Remove and spread on plate. Heat 1 tablespoon oil, add mushrooms and water chestnuts; stir-fry until heated through. Remove to plate. Heat remaining oil, add ginger and garlic, color lightly. Stir in beef mixture, turning constantly until almost done (or cook meat in batches, setting each aside as cooked). Remove ginger slice. Add cooked vegetables; simply heat through, do not cook. Taste for seasoning. Serve immediately.

*Available at specialty food stores.

Makes 8 servings.

CHINESE LETTUCE APPETIZERS

As appealing to look at as to taste. Serve as an appetizer, a luncheon main dish or as a salad with an Oriental dinner.

```
   1 clove garlic, peeled
   1 can (8 ounces) water chestnuts, drained
   1 can (3-1/2 ounces) colossal-size smoked oysters, drained
  10 scallions, cut in thirds
   2 large (1 pound) boneless skinned chicken breasts, cut in pieces
     to fit feed tube, then frozen
  32 leaves Bibb lettuce
  16 to 24 leaves Boston lettuce
   4 cups peanut oil
   3 ounces bean thread noodles
 1/3 cup walnuts
   2 cups bean sprouts, fresh or well drained, if canned
```

Sauce

```
   2 tablespoons light soy sauce*
   4 tablespoons oyster sauce*
 1/2 teaspoon sugar
 1/2 teaspoon cayenne pepper
   3 tablespoons dry sherry
   1 teaspoon sesame oil
```

As you process the following ingredients, set them aside in separate bowls. Steel Knife: Mince garlic (drop through feed tube while machine is running). With on/off turns, chop water chestnuts, then oysters, both coarsely. Serrated Slicer: Wedge scallions vertically in feed tube, slice -- light pressure. Slice slightly defrosted chicken breasts. Firm pressure.

Place lettuce leaves in a circle around edge of large platter. Heat oil in a wok to deep-fry temperature. (Test with a piece of noodle -- if it pops up immediately, oil is hot). Deep fry noodles; when puffed up, turn to cook on other side. Drain well on paper towels. Break into smaller serving pieces and mound in center of platter. Deep fry walnuts in same hot oil and drain on paper towels.

Steel Knife: Chop nuts coarsely. Remove all but 2 tablespoons oil from wok. Heat oil, cook garlic and scallions (all but 2 tablespoons for garnish) lightly. Add chicken and stir-fry until chicken is opaque. Add oysters; stir-fry with chicken for a minute. Add water chestnuts and bean sprouts. Stir together sauce ingredients; add to chicken mixture and stir well. Taste for seasoning (soy sauce or salt); place on the

(continued on other side)

CHINESE LETTUCE APPETIZERS (cont.)

noodles. Garnish with walnuts and reserved scallion slices. Serve hot, wrapping mixture with noodles in a lettuce leaf.

*Available at specialty food stores.

Makes 8 servings.

CHINESE NOODLES SUPREME

Crunchy texture and delicate taste.

Sauce

3/4 cup chicken broth
1 tablespoon sugar
3 tablespoons soy sauce

6 dried Chinese mushrooms
10 ounces Chinese noodles
1 tablespoon sesame oil
2 cloves garlic, peeled
3/4 pound boneless pork, cut in 1-inch cubes
1 pound bok choy (2 cups sliced)
12 scallions, cut in 2-inch lengths (1 cup slivered)
2 cups fresh or canned bean sprouts
1/4 cup dry sherry

Combine sauce ingredients; set aside.

Soak mushrooms in warm water until spongy -- about 30 minutes. Cut off stems (reserve for another use). Bring 4 quarts unsalted water to boil, add noodles, cook about 5 minutes until softened; drain, rinse immediately with cold water, drain well, toss with sesame oil.

Set aside following ingredients as processed. Steel Knife: Mince garlic (drop through feed tube with machine running). Chop pork -- on/off turns until desired size. Serrated Slicer: Wedge bok choy vertically in feed tube, slice -- medium pressure. Lay scallions horizontally in feed tube, slice to feather or sliver -- light pressure. Shredder: Shred mushroom caps.

Pour boiling water over bean sprouts. Let stand 2 minutes, blanch under cold water until cold, drain. Heat oil in wok, add garlic, allow to color lightly. Add pork, stir-fry 6 minutes or until completely cooked. Add sherry, mix well. Add 1/2 of scallions, bok choy, bean sprouts; stir until heated through. Add sauce and noodles. Turn heat to medium, stir for 2 minutes. Place on serving platter; garnish with remaining slivered scallions.

Makes 8 servings.

JAPANESE RELISH

Two keys to success: be sure to blanch the cabbage, and to refrigerate at least overnight before serving.

Dressing

    1 slice (1 inch) fresh ginger, peeled*
1-1/4 cups rice vinegar
    6 tablespoons sugar
    1 teaspoon Lawry's seasoning pepper

1-1/2 pounds cabbage, cut in wedges to fit feed tube
      (5 cups sliced)
   1 tablespoon salt
  16 radishes
  12 scallions, cut in half lengthwise
   1 medium cucumber
   1 medium red or green pepper, seeded
   2 turnips, peeled
   3 large carrots, peeled and cut in 2-inch lengths
 1/2 cup Japanese pickle radishes, drained (optional)

Steel Knife: Grate ginger (with machine running, drop ginger through feed tube). Remove and set aside.

Heat rice vinegar and sugar together until sugar is dissolved. Add Lawry's pepper and ginger; set aside.

Serrated Slicer: Slice cabbage. Place cabbage in large pot, pour boiling water over cabbage, add salt. Let stand 10 minutes. Drain, blanch immediately in cold water, drain well. Slice radishes, scallions (place in vertical compact bunches in feed tube), cucumber, red or green pepper (if too large to fit feed tube from bottom, cut one side open -- roll pepper into tight coil so when sliced, it will appear as a whole ring to be used as a garnish).

To make julienne or matchstick turnips, trim turnips to largest size that will fit feed tube; slice once, firm pressure. Hold cover upside down, insert pusher to leave a cup an inch deep at the bottom of feed tube. Make a compact group of slices in this cup so turnips will not fall out when cover is placed back on bowl; slice, firm pressure. Repeat with remaining slices.
Shredder: Place carrots in feed tube in horizontal stack; shred, firm pressure.

Mix dressing with vegetables. Let marinate overnight -- will last 4 days, covered and refrigerated. Serve as a relish in small individual bowls.

*Use a vegetable peeler to peel ginger (semi-frozen) before cutting off 1 inch piece.

Makes 8 servings.

APRICOT MOUSSE IN ORANGE SHELLS

My students loved this -- in part because it can be made in advance, but mainly for its delicate taste.

    Zest of 2 oranges, removed in strips with sharp vegetable peeler
- 1 cup sugar
- 8 ounces dried apricots (about 1-1/2 cups)
- 1 cup orange juice
- 3/4 cup water
- 1 teaspoon fresh lemon juice
- 4 USDA large egg yolks
- 1 cup warm milk
- 1 envelope unflavored gelatin, softened in 3 tablespoons Grand Marnier
- 1 teaspoon vanilla
- 5 USDA large egg whites
- 1 cup heavy cream, whipped <u>or</u>
- 3/4 cup Crème Fraîche (see basic recipe)
- 8 to 12 oranges, scooped out
- 1/2 cup heavy cream
- 1 tablespoon sugar
- 1 tablespoon Grand Marnier

<u>Steel Knife</u>: Place orange zest strips and 1/2 cup sugar in bowl, let machine run until zest is minced. Mix with apricots, orange juice, water and lemon juice. Let soak 1/2 hour. Cook <u>slowly</u>, covered, 1/2 hour or until apricots are soft.

<u>Plastic Knife</u>: Place 1/2 cup sugar and egg yolks in bowl, let machine run until mixture is pale yellow and thick. Place in top of double boiler, pour in warm milk, cook custard until mixture coats a spoon. Add softened gelatine mixture and vanilla -- stir until dissolved.

With electric beater, beat egg whites until stiff, <u>not dry</u>. Add 1/4 egg whites to warm, not hot, mixture. Fold thoroughly (this lightens basic mixture -- egg whites are poached slightly and remain puffy). Add this mixture to remaining egg whites; fold them together as lightly as possible. Chill mixture until it starts to set.

<u>Steel Knife</u>: Purée apricot mixture -- let machine run until puréed -- can be coarse or smooth. Combine purée in a mixing bowl with whipped cream or Crème Fraîche. Fold into chilled mixture. Spoon mousse into a glass bowl or prepared orange shells (cut flat bottoms, cut 1/2 inch off top -- scoop orange out carefully with grapefruit spoon or small sharp knife). Chill. When firm, whip 1/2 cup cream, flavor with sugar and Grand Marnier -- fill pastry bag fitted with a medium star tube and decorate. If available, mint leaves add a fresh, natural garnish.

Makes 8 to 12 servings.

SABLES

In a cooking school in Paris, the instructor made the dough for these delicious sugar cookies by hand. It took 15 minutes. The Cuisinart food processor does it in less than a minute.

```
    3 hard-cooked egg yolks
1-1/2 cups unbleached all-purpose flour
  1/4 cup cake flour
      Pinch salt
    1 cup confectioners sugar
  1/2 pound (2 sticks) chilled unsalted butter, each
      cut in 6 pieces
      Zest of 1 lemon (or orange)
  1/2 teaspoon lemon extract
    1 teaspoon water
```

Glaze

```
    1 egg
  1/2 teaspoon salt
```

Steel Knife: Chop egg yolks until they appear sieved. Add flours, salt, sugar, butter, lemon zest, lemon extract and water. Turn machine on/off several times, then let run until mixture is blended. Wrap and chill at least 30 minutes.

Preheat oven to 375 degrees. Grease 2 baking sheets, splash sparsely with water. Divide dough into thirds, leaving unworked dough in refrigerator until ready to roll.

Roll out dough to 1/4 inch thickness, stamp out rounds using a 1-1/2-inch cookie cutter. Place on baking sheet. Plastic Knife: Mix egg and salt -- 4 quick on/off turns. Brush cookies with glaze and mark a triangle on each with a fork. Chill 10 to 15 minutes, then bake 10 to 12 minutes or until lightly browned. Do not overbake. Transfer to wire rack to cool.

Makes 30 1-1/2-inch cookies.

AN INDIAN MEAL

Zucchini and Tomato Soup

* * *

Salmon Pâté

* * *

Lamb Curry

Saffron Rice

Condiment Tray

* * *

Yogurt Cucumber Salad

Red Lentil Relish

* * *

Fresh Strawberry Tart

ZUCCHINI AND TOMATO SOUP

Serve hot or cold. This recipe will launch you into the flourless world of thickening all soups with vegetable purées.

1/4 cup parsley leaves, firmly packed (1/8 cup minced)
  1 tablespoon snipped chives
  2 medium onions, peeled and quartered (1-1/2 cups minced)
  2 large tomatoes, peeled, seeded, quartered (3/4 cup coarsely chopped)
  6 small unpeeled zucchini
  1 teaspoon salt
  2 tablespoons oil
  4 cups chicken stock
1/2 teaspoon sugar
1/2 teaspoon oregano
1/2 teaspoon basil
  2 teaspoons lemon juice
  Salt
  Freshly ground black pepper
  Freshly grated nutmeg

Steel Knife: Mince parsley and chives together -- quick on/off turns; reserve for garnish. Mince onions -- quick on/off turns, set aside. Chop tomatoes coarsely -- quick on/off turns. Set aside.

Serrated Slicer: Slice zucchini by placing vertically in feed tube, medium pressure. Reserve 8 slices for garnish. Sprinkle remaining zucchini with salt. Drain in colander for 30 minutes; pat dry with paper towel.

In large pot, heat oil; add onion and zucchini, cover and sauté slowly 10 minutes. Add stock and simmer 20 minutes. Steel Knife: Remove zucchini and onions from stock; purée. Return to pot, add tomatoes, sugar, oregano, basil, lemon juice and salt, pepper and nutmeg to taste; cook 5 minutes. If soup is too thick, thin with additional stock or with cream or milk. Serve hot or chilled. Garnish with zucchini slices, parsley and chives.

Makes 8 servings.

SALMON PATE

An ideal spread to have on hand. It keeps, refrigerated, for at least 10 days.

```
  1 small onion, peeled and quartered (1/4 cup minced)
  1 can (1 pound) red salmon, skinned and boned (drain some liquid from can)
  1 package (8 ounces) cream cheese, softened
  2 to 3 tablespoons lemon juice
  1 generous tablespoon horseradish
  2 teaspoons dried dill
1/4 cup parsley leaves, firmly packed (1/8 cup minced)
1/4 teaspoon liquid smoke
    Dash Tabasco
  1 teaspoon Worcestershire
    Salt
    Freshly ground black pepper
```

Steel Knife: Mince onion -- quick on/off turns. Add remaining ingredients to bowl, blend with quick on/off turns, then let run until smooth. Adjust seasonings by increasing proportions of spicy ingredients, if desired. Refrigerate overnight.

Serve on raw vegetable slices. Serrated Slicer: Slice kohlrabi, cucumbers, turnips, etc. Otherwise, thin slices of pumpernickel are recommended. The mixture can be shaped into a mound and garnished with minced parsley and/or chopped nuts.

Makes 2 cups.

SAFFRON RICE

This go-with speaks for itself. My favorite rice is Basmati. It comes from India and is used the world over, especially by many French chefs, because it holds its long, thin shape.

```
  1/4 cup parsley leaves, firmly packed (1/8 cup minced)
    3 cups water
    3 tablespoons butter
1-1/2 cups rice
    2 teaspoons salt
      Pinch saffron threads
    1 stick (2 inches) cinnamon
```

<u>Steel Knife</u>: Mince parsley -- quick on/off turns, reserve. Bring all ingredients except parsley to boil. Stir through. Let simmer, covered, over low heat for 15 minutes or until liquid is absorbed. Do not stir, but check liquid by tilting pan and lifting rice with a fork. When liquid is absorbed, set aside, covered, for an additional 10 minutes to complete the cooking. Fluff rice with a fork. Check seasoning. Can be prepared in advance, left uncovered to cool, then reheated in double boiler.

Makes 8 servings.

LAMB CURRY

Vegetables and fruit are used instead of flour to thicken the sauce. The sauce can be made well in advance. In fact, it improves with standing for several days.

- 1/4 cup parsley leaves, firmly packed (1/8 cup minced)
- 2 cloves garlic, peeled
- 3 large onions, peeled and quartered (3 cups minced)
- 2 tablespoons butter
- 2 small apples, unpeeled, quartered and cored (1 cup chopped)
- 1 large carrot (1 cup chopped)
- 1 large celery stalk (1 cup sliced)
- 1/2 teaspoon curry powder (or to taste)
- 3 cups beef stock
- 2 tablespoons beef stock base, if desired
- 1/2 cup dry vermouth
- 2 tablespoons tomato paste
- 2 tablespoons lemon juice
- 2 cardamom seeds, crushed
- 1/2 cup currants
- 1/4 teaspoon thyme
- 1 bay leaf
- 2 tablespoons cream of coconut*
- 1 cup yogurt
- 4 pounds lamb from the leg, cut in 1-1/2 inch cubes
- Salt
- Freshly ground black pepper
- 2 tablespoons butter
- 2 tablespoons oil

<u>Steel Knife</u>: Mince parsley -- quick on/off turns, reserve for garnish. Mince garlic, onions together -- quick on/off turns. Empty into large pot with 2 tablespoons butter; cover, cook until limp -- about 10 minutes. Chop apples -- quick on/off turns. Repeat with carrots. <u>Serrated Slicer</u>: Slice celery. Add curry powder to onion and garlic; cook slowly 5 minutes. Add remaining ingredients (except meat, butter, oil, salt, pepper), simmer 1 hour.

Sprinkle meat (patted dry with paper towels) with salt, freshly ground black pepper; sear in small batches in 2 tablespoons butter and oil (this must be done rapidly over high heat). Combine meat with curry sauce, heat through (do not cook). Adjust seasoning with salt and pepper, sprinkle with reserved parsley. Beef (sirloin tip), chicken or shrimp can be substituted for the lamb, but remember never to overcook your choice in the final reheating. This curry sauce is excellent for leftovers, too.

(continued on other side)

LAMB CURRY (cont.)

* Available in ethnic food stores -- or make your own by placing freshly grated coconut in juice from coconut and enough milk to equal 1 cup. Bring to boil, let stand 30 minutes, strain -- use 1/4 cup as substitute for cream of coconut in recipe.

Makes 8 servings.

CURRY CONDIMENT TRAY

Choose your own favorites. Many can be prepared in advance. Keep in mind the platter on which they will finally end up so that you can produce a picture of contrasting textures and colors as well as tastes.

1. Ten slices bacon, well cooked, drained. <u>Steel Knife</u>: Crumble bacon -- quick on/off turns.

2. Chutney selections.

3. One cup peanuts. <u>Steel Knife</u>: Chop coarsely -- quick on/off turns.

4. Whites of 3 hard-cooked eggs. <u>Steel Knife</u>: Chop coarsely -- quick on/off turns.

5. Yolks of 3 hard-cooked eggs. <u>Steel Knife</u>: Chop egg yolks -- quick on/off turns.

6. One large green pepper, seeded. <u>Serrated Slicer</u>: Slice. <u>Steel Knife</u>: Mince slices in 2 batches -- quick on/off turns (as few as possible).

7. One coconut. Crack, peel, cut to fit feed tube. <u>Shredder</u>: Shred, using firm pressure.

8. One cup seedless green grapes. <u>Serrated Slicer</u>: Directly on blade, place a base of grapes with ends cut flat; begin to pyramid others on this base. Carefully set cover on machine. Place remaining grapes in feed tube -- slice with light pressure.

9. One cup sweet pickle slices. <u>Serrated Slicer</u>: Slice into matchsticks (see Yogurt Cucumber Salad for method).

10. One large banana. <u>Serrated Slicer</u>: Cut banana into lengths to fit vertically into feed tube -- quarter lengthwise; place in feed tube -- slice with light pressure. Mix with 1 tablespoon lemon juice.

11. One avocado, peeled. Dice with knife on cutting board. Mix with 1 tablespoon lemon juice.

12. Three-fourths cup pinenuts, sautéed until golden in 1 tablespoon oil.

YOGURT CUCUMBER SALAD

1/2 cup parsley leaves, firmly packed (1/4 cup minced)
  1 shallot, peeled
  2 large firm cucumbers, unpeeled
  1 cup yogurt
  1 tablespoon dried dill weed
    Salt
    Freshly ground black pepper

Steel Knife: Mince parsley -- quick on/off turns, reserve. Mince shallot -- drop through feed tube with machine running. Remove and set aside. Serrated Slicer: Slice cucumbers, empty from bowl. To make a true julienne cut -- hold bowl cover upside down, remove pusher to form a 1-inch cup -- wedge cucumber slices together compactly enough so they will not fall out when cover is replaced. Slice. Drain in colander. At serving time, mix with all remaining ingredients; garnish with minced parsley.

Makes about 4 cups.

RED OR ORANGE LENTIL RELISH

  1 cup red or orange lentils
  1 clove garlic, unpeeled
  1 small onion, unpeeled
1/4 cup parsley leaves, firmly packed (1/8 cup minced)
  2 shallots, peeled
  6 tablespoons oil
  2 tablespoons lime juice
    Salt
    Freshly ground black pepper

Wash lentils, cook in water to cover with garlic and onion until tender, nut mushy -- about 12 minutes. Watch carefully, drain. Remove garlic and onion. Steel Knife: Mince parsley -- quick on/off turns, reserve. Mince shallots -- drop through feed tube with machine running. Mix shallots with oil, lime juice, salt and pepper to taste. Mix warm, drained lentils in marinade; refrigerate. Garnish with parsley.

Makes 1-1/2 cups.

FRESH STRAWBERRY TART

The crust and crème can be prepared in advance, and final assembling is easy.

Pâte Brisée

- 1-1/2 cups unbleached all-purpose flour
- 2 tablespoons sugar
- Pinch salt
- 1 USDA large egg yolk
- 4 ounces (1 stick) chilled unsalted butter, cut in 6 pieces
- 5 tablespoons ice water

Crème Pâtissière

- 1/4 cup natural whole almonds, blanched
- 1 cup milk
- 3 USDA large egg yolks
- 1/4 cup sugar
- 1/4 cup Wondra flour
- 1 tablespoon Kirsch

Glaze

- 1 cup apricot preserves or currant jelly
- 1 tablespoon Kirsch
- 1 tablespoon water

3 pints uniform-size strawberries, hulled.

Pâte Brisée. Steel Knife: Place flour, sugar, salt and egg yolk in bowl. Turn machine on/off to combine ingredients. Add butter. Turn machine on/off until mixture resembles coarse meal. With machine running, pour ice water through feed tube. As soon as dough forms a ball, remove, press flat, wrap in plastic, chill at least 2 hours. Roll out on lightly floured board, place in lightly buttered 11-inch quiche pan or flan, prick bottom and sides with a fork; refrigerate 30 minutes. Line with parchment paper, fill with beans or rice, bake in preheated 400 degree oven 12 minutes. Remove paper and beans, prick crust again, bake 10 minutes longer or until crust is well baked and browned. Watch carefully so it doesn't burn. Let cool on wire rack.

Crème Pâtissière. Steel Knife: Chop almonds coarsely -- quick on/off turns. Reserve. Heat milk. Plastic Knife: Combine egg yolks and sugar until thick and light colored. Add flour and blend well. Add heated milk through

(continued on other side)

FRESH STRAWBERRY TART (cont.)

feed tube with machine running, combine well. Return to saucepan, cook until very thick, stirring constantly. Add Kirsch and almonds. Cool.

Glaze. Heat preserves with Kirsch and water until melted -- strain through sieve. Brush bottom of baked crust with glaze. Wait 5 minutes.

Spread Crème Pâtissière no more than 1/2 inch thick on crust. Any excess crème can be frozen. Arrange strawberries, placing them with points toward center and starting at outer edge. Brush with glaze. Serve the tart plain, with Crème Chantilly (1/2 cup lightly whipped cream mixed with 1/2 cup Crème Fraîche -- see basic recipe, sweetened and flavored with vanilla) or with vanilla-flavored and sweetened whipped cream. Do not assemble tart more than 3 hours in advance of serving.

Makes 8 servings.

A PARISIAN DINNER

Fish Pâté au Cresson

Hollandaise au Cresson

Mayonnaise au Cresson

or

Hummous, Romaine Leaves

* * *

Herbed Leg of Lamb

Tian of Eggplant and Rice

Cucumbers à la Grecque

* * *

Pain Complet - Whole Wheat Bread

* * *

French Cream Cheese Cake, Strawberry Sauce

or

Mixed Fruit Clafouti

HUMMOUS

If you want to cut down on calories, spread the hummous on tender leaves of romaine lettuce instead of warmed wedges of pita bread.

```
  1 clove garlic, peeled
  1 small onion, peeled and quartered
1/2 cup parsley leaves, firmly packed (1/4 cup minced)
  1 can (20 ounces) chick peas, drained
1/2 cup Tahini paste
  1 tablespoon dried cilantro*
  1 tablespoon fresh lemon juice
  1 teaspoon red wine vinegar
    Dash Tabasco
1/8 cup oil
1/4 cup water
    Salt
    Romaine lettuce leaves or
    Pita bread
```

Steel Knife: Mince garlic (drop through feed tube with machine running). Mince onion -- quick on/off turns. Add remaining ingredients; turn machine on/off 4 times to blend, then let it run until mixture is puréed. Taste for seasoning; adjust, add more water if necessary. Serve spread on leaves of romaine or on warmed pita bread wedges.

*Known also as Chinese parsley or coriander leaf. It resembles flat-leaf Italian parsley in appearance. The Spanish name is cilantro.

Makes about 2 cups.

FISH PATE AU CRESSON

This fish pâté was inspired by one served at Le Pactole, a very innovative restaurant and the top-rated bistro in France. Most restaurants serve their fish pâtés hot with a light hollandaise sauce, but others prefer to present it cold with mayonnaise. You will find both sauce recipes here, so take your choice.

      1 cup watercress leaves and stems, firmly packed
      8 sole fillets, about 2 pounds
      1 tablespoon lemon juice
      2 shallots, peeled
    1-1/2 pounds salmon (after boning, skinning),
          cut in 2-inch pieces
      4 large USDA egg whites
      3/4 cup whipping cream or
      1 cup Crème Fraîche (see basic recipe)
          Dash Tabasco
          Salt
          Freshly ground white pepper
      1/4 teaspoon freshly grated nutmeg
      1 lemon, scored
      1 small red pepper, seeded
          Watercress sprigs

Sauces

    Hollandaise au Cresson (recipe follows)
    Mayonnaise au Cresson (recipe follows)

Preheat oven to 375 degrees. Cut parchment paper to fit bottom of a 6-cup terrine or loaf pan; butter side of paper that faces up. Butter sides of terrine or loaf pan. Place watercress in boiling, salted water 1 minute, drain, refresh in cold water; drain thoroughly. Squeeze dry with paper towels; set aside. Wash fillets in cold water to cover and lemon juice. Dry with paper towels.

Steel Knife: Mince shallots (drop through feed tube with machine running), leave in bowl. Add few pieces of salmon at a time; purée by letting machine run -- repeat until all fish is puréed. Add egg whites; let machine run until mixture is totally blended. Add cream or Crème Fraîche. Blend thoroughly. Add Tabasco. Season generously with salt and pepper (mixture can be tested by dropping spoonful into boiling water -- adjust seasoning accordingly). Remove all but 5 tablespoons purée from work bowl -- add watercress; purée by letting machine run.

Assembly: Line prepared terrine or loaf pan with fillets, covering all

(continued on other side)

FISH PATE AU CRESSON (cont.)

sides of terrine. Spread half of pâté mixture into terrine; lay a fillet down the middle. Spoon in dollops of watercress mixture in an irregular pattern, wedging the salmon pâté mixture in between each dollop. Spread remaining pâté mixture over this. Bang terrine down to settle contents solidly. Cover with well-buttered parchment paper. Pâté can be prepared in advance. Set in water bath (bain-marie), measuring at least 1/2 way up on terrine. Bring to boil on top of stove; bake in preheated 375 degree oven 45 minutes. Drain off liquid. Let rest 10 minutes in terrine -- invert onto platter. <u>Garnish</u>. <u>Serrated Slicer</u>: Slice scored lemon, ends cut off, using firm pressure. Slice red pepper, using light pressure. Serve hot with Hollandaise au Cresson or cold with Mayonnaise au Cresson.

Makes 8 to 14 servings.

HOLLANDAISE AU CRESSON

  3 USDA large egg yolks
  1 tablespoon lemon juice
1/2 teaspoon salt
1/2 teaspoon white pepper
  4 ounces (1 stick) butter, melted
1/4 cup watercress leaves, blanched 30 seconds in
    boiling water, refreshed in cold water, squeezed dry

<u>Steel Knife</u>: Place egg yolks, lemon juice, salt, pepper in work bowl -- quick on/off turns to blend. Through feed tube, with machine running, pour in melted butter in slow stream. When thickened, add watercress -- quick on/off -- adjust seasoning.

Makes 1-1/8 cup.

MAYONNAISE AU CRESSON

<u>Steel Knife</u>: Place 1-1/2 cups Basic Mayonnaise (see page   ), 1 cup watercress leaves and stems (firmly packed) in bowl -- turn on/off until watercress is puréed into mayonnaise. Adjust seasoning.

Makes 1-3/4 cups.

HERBED LEG OF LAMB

A lamb recipe in the French tradition. Important: for the pink of perfection use a professional <u>instant reading</u> meat thermometer. There is no other way to be sure the <u>lamb will be right</u>.

```
    1 leg of lamb, 6 to 8 pounds
    2 cloves garlic, slivered
   16 fresh sprigs  parsley, basil, mint (use only parsley
      if that is all that is available)
    1 medium carrot, unpeeled and cut in 2-inch pieces
    2 medium onions, peeled and halved
    1 cup brown stock
    2 cups dry red wine
  1/2 cup oil
    2 teaspoons salt
    1 teaspoon oregano
    1 teaspoon basil
      Parsley
      Cherry tomatoes
```

Wipe lamb clean. With point of small knife, insert garlic, parsley, basil, mint (it looks beautiful). <u>Steel Knife</u>: Chop carrot -- quick on/off turns. <u>Serrated Slicer</u>: Slice onions. Mix carrot and onions with remaining ingredients and pour over meat in large bowl. Marinate in refrigerator overnight, turning occasionally.

After removing from refrigerator, let stand until room temperature. Remove from marinade and place in pan in preheated 400 degree oven. Brown 15 to 20 minutes. Pour marinade over meat and roast until pink -- 147 degrees -- about 20 minutes per pound, basting occasionally. Remove meat from pan and let rest 20 minutes. Skim marinade and simmer until reduced about 1/2. <u>Steel Knife</u>: Purée sauce in 2 or 3 batches. Glaze meat with a little of the sauce and garnish platter with parsley and tomatoes. Pass balance of sauce.

Makes 8 to 10 servings.

TIAN OF EGGPLANT AND RICE

This casserole can also be made with zucchini.

```
     2 ounces Parmesan cheese (1/2 cup shredded)
     2 ounces mozzarella cheese (1/2 cup shredded)
 1-1/2 pounds eggplant, unpeeled, cut in largest size
         wedges to fit feed tube (7 cups sliced)
     2 teaspoons salt
   1/2 slice bread (1/4 cup bread crumbs)
   1/4 cup parsley leaves, firmly packed (1/8 cup minced)
     1 clove garlic, peeled
     1 medium onion, peeled and quartered (1/4 cup minced)
     3 medium tomatoes, peeled and seeded (3/4 cup coarsely chopped)
     2 tablespoons butter
     2 tablespoons oil
     1 cup cooked rice
       Salt
       Freshly ground black pepper
   1/4 cup pinenuts sautéed in 1 tablespoon butter (optional)
```

Shredder: Shred cheeses (Parmesan at room temperature, mozzarella chilled, using light pressure on both. Set aside.

Serrated Slicer: Slice eggplant, place in colander, sprinkle with salt; let stand 30 minutes to drain, pat completely dry with paper towels.
Steel Knife: Mince bread and parsley -- quick on/off turns, set aside. Mince garlic (drop through feed tube with machine running), leave in work bowl -- mince onion -- quick on/off turns. Set aside. Chop prepared tomatoes in batches coarsely -- quick on/off turns.

Sauté garlic and onion in butter and oil until very soft, not brown. When onion is soft, add prepared eggplant, cover, steam through, shake pan to mix. Add tomatoes, simmer 3 minutes; stir in rice, minced parsley, salt and pepper to taste, 1/4 cup grated cheeses. Turn into 6-cup buttered ovenproof dish -- sprinkle with crumbs, remaining cheeses, sautéed pinenuts. Bake in preheated 375 degree oven 40 minutes or until browned and bubbly.

Note: If substituting zucchini for the eggplant, use 2-1/4 pounds (6-3/4 cups sliced).

Makes 8 servings.

CUCUMBERS A LA GRECQUE

You may substitute your own herb seasoning for the Cavender's in this cucumber salad.

```
   1/2 cup parsley leaves, firmly packed (1/4 cup minced)
     1 tablespoon fresh dill or
 1-1/2 teaspoons dried dill weed
     8 to 10 pickle-size cucumbers (each about 5 inches long) or
     2 large cucumbers, unpeeled (4 cups sliced)
     1 small red onion, peeled (1/3 cup sliced)
     8 Calamata olives (optional)*
```

Dressing

```
   3/4 cup oil
   1/4 cup red wine vinegar
     2 tablespoons Cavender's Greek Seasoning*
   1/2 teaspoon salt
       Freshly ground black pepper
```

Steel Knife: Mince parsley and dill together (it refreshes the dried dill). Serrated Slicer: Score, cut cucumbers to fit feed tube. Slice, using medium pressure. Slice onion, using firm pressure. Remove from bowl.

Plastic Knife: Mix salad dressing -- quick on/off turns. Use about 2/3 cup in salad -- mix all salad ingredients together with dressing.

*Available at ethnic specialty stores.

Makes 8 servings.

PAIN COMPLET
(Whole Wheat Bread)

One experiment finally paid off in my search for a way to reproduce the texture of fine French bread. What does the trick is introducing cake flour into a bread dough.

Glaze

    1 USDA large egg
1/2 teaspoon salt

    2 tablespoons honey
    1 package active dry yeast
1-1/8 cups warm water (105 to 115 degrees)
1-1/2 cups stone ground whole wheat flour
1-1/2 cups cake flour
  1/8 cup oil
1-1/2 teaspoons salt

Plastic Knife: Mix egg and salt -- 4 quick on/off turns. Set aside, covered and refrigerated.

Add honey and yeast to warm water; proof. Mix flours together. Steel Knife: Place 2 cups flour, oil and salt in bowl -- add 1/2 cup liquid, turn machine on/off 4 times. Add balance of liquid, repeating on/off motion. Add 3/4 cup remaining flour, repeat on/off motion 4 times, then leave machine on until dough forms a ball. Stop machine, touch dough, and if too sticky (should be slightly sticky), add flour. Let machine run to knead dough -- until smooth and slightly sticky to the touch (no more than 60 seconds).

Place in lightly oiled bowl, turning dough so oiled all over, cover with damp towel and put in warm place (about 80 degrees) until doubled in bulk -- about 1 to 1-1/2 hours. Remove to lightly floured board and roll out to rectangle, the length of the pan. Form loaf, pinch seam, press ends and tuck under tightly. Put in oiled 9- or 10-inch loaf pan, seam down. Cover with a damp cloth, let double again in a warm place -- about 60 minutes.

Preheat oven to 375 degrees. Brush loaf with egg glaze, bake 50 to 60 minutes or until it sounds hollow when tapped on the bottom. Turn out on a wire rack to cool.

Makes a 9- or 10-inch loaf.

83

FRENCH CREAM CHEESE CAKE, STRAWBERRY SAUCE

A new version of a truly American dessert which appeared in France only recently. The strawberry sauce is more delicate and elegant than the usual American fruit topping.

Crust

- 1 package (7 ounces) Petit Beurre Biscuits or vanilla wafers (2 cups crumbs)
- 1 stick unsalted butter, melted
- 3 tablespoons sugar
- 1 teaspoon cinnamon
- 1/2 teaspoon freshly grated nutmeg

Filling

- 2 packages (8 ounces each) cream cheese, softened or if chilled, cut each in 3 pieces
- 4 USDA large eggs, separated
- 1 cup heavy cream
- 3/4 cup sugar
- 2 teaspoons fresh lemon juice
- 1/2 teaspoon lemon zest
- 1 tablespoon flour
- 1/4 teaspoon salt
- 1-1/2 teaspoons vanilla

Sauce

- 1 pint fresh strawberries, hulled
- 2 tablespoons sugar
- 1/8 cup imported Kirsch
- 1 package (10 ounces) frozen raspberries, defrosted

Crust. Preheat oven to 300 degrees. Lightly butter a 9-inch springform pan. Steel Knife: Place 1/2 the biscuits or wafers in bowl -- turn on/off 4 times, then let machine run until desired-size crumbs. Remove. Repeat procedure with remaining biscuits. Return all crumbs to work bowl -- add butter, sugar and spices -- blend with quick on/off turns. Press crumbs around bottom and 2 inches up on sides of springform pan.

Filling. Steel Knife: Place cream cheese, egg yolks in bowl -- make 4 quick on/off turns, then let machine run until blended. Add cream, sugar, lemon juice, lemon zest, flour, salt and vanilla -- blend thoroughly with 8 quick on/off turns. Pour into mixing bowl. Beat egg whites with electric mixer or rotary beater until stiff. Fold 1/4 egg whites into cream mixture, then fold this mixture

(continued on other side)

FRENCH CREAM CHEESE CAKE, STRAWBERRY SAUCE (cont.)

into remaining egg whites; folding gently. Pour into crust; wrap base of springform pan with heavy duty foil; place in water bath (bain-marie), bring to boil on top of stove, then bake for 2 hours, turn off oven and leave in another hour with oven door closed. Serve either at room temperature or cold with strawberry sauce.

Sauce. Serrated Slicer: Slice strawberries, using light pressure. Mix with sugar, Kirsch -- let stand 1 hour. Steel Knife: Add raspberries -- let machine run until puréed; sieve, pour over prepared strawberries.

Makes 8 to 12 servings.

MIXED FRUIT CLAFOUTI

The traditional clafouti uses only cherries. I prefer this more varied and colorful version.

1/3 cup sugar
    Zest of 1 lemon, cut in strips with vegetable peeler
4 cups mixed prepared fruit (sliced apples, peaches, plums; pitted cherries, blueberries)
1 teaspoon lemon juice
1/4 cup Cognac

Batter

1/2 cup unbleached all-purpose flour
1/3 cup sugar
1/8 teaspoon salt
3 USDA large eggs
    Reserved fruit liquid plus enough milk to measure 1-1/4 cups
2 tablespoons vanilla extract
    Cinnamon
    Confectioners sugar

Steel Knife: Place 1/3 cup sugar and lemon zest strips in work bowl -- 6 on/off turns, then let machine run until zest is minced. Serrated Slicer: Slice apples, peaches or plums, placing fruit horizontally in feed tube. Regulate slicing pressure according to texture of fruit (medium pressure, apple; light pressure, peach). Mix fruit and sugar-zest mixture with lemon juice and Cognac; let stand 1/2 hour. Drain fruit, using this liquid and enough milk to measure 1-1/2 cups.

Plastic Knife: Add flour, sugar, salt, eggs to work bowl -- 6 on/off turns. With machine running, pour milk mixture and vanilla gradually through feed tube; process until smooth. Butter a 9- or 10-inch quiche dish, place drained fruit, evenly distributed, on bottom. Pour batter over top. Sprinkle generously with cinnamon. Bake in preheated 350 degree oven for 1 hour or until browned and puffy. Serve warm or at room temperature. Sprinkle with sieved confectioners sugar. Serve with Vanilla Sauce (see basic recipes).

Makes 6 servings.

NOTES

A SCALLOP DINNER

Pissaladière Nicoise

or

Onion-Parmesan Appetizers

* * *

Baked Scallops aux Herbes

Vegetable Pâté

Tomato Sauce

* * *

Julienned Beet Salad, Mimosa

Mustard Vinaigrette Dressing

* * *

Quick Pain de Mie

* * *

Boule de Neige

or

Sliced Pineapple in Kirsch

ONION PARMESAN APPETIZERS

This spread is delicious on thin-sliced homemade Pain de Mie (see recipe page 95). Or spread on fish fillets, then bake or broil until bubbly and brown.

```
  3 ounces Parmesan cheese (3/4 cup shredded)
  1 medium onion, peeled (3/4 cup minced)
3/4 cup mayonnaise (see basic recipe)
    Paprika, preferably Hungarian
 24 small bread rounds, about 1-3/4 inches, or
    Pain de Mie, thinly sliced and quartered
```

Shredder: Shred cheese (must be at room temperature -- remember the "knife test" explained in techniques section), using light pressure. Set aside. Steel Knife: Mince onion -- quick on/off turns. Mix together shredded cheese, minced onion, mayonnaise and paprike to taste. Spread on bread rounds or thinly sliced, quartered Pain de Mie. Broil until puffy and browned, about 5 minutes.

Makes 24 appetizers.

PISSALADIERE NICOISE
(French Pizza)

This is the French counterpart of the Italian pizza.

Dough

1/2 package active dry yeast (1 teaspoon)
1/2 cup warm water (105 to 115 degrees)
1/2 teaspoon sugar
  1 cup plus 3 tablespoons unbleached flour
1/2 teaspoon salt
1/2 teaspoon oil

Topping

1/2 cup parsley leaves, firmly packed (1/4 cup minced)
  3 large onions, peeled and quartered (3 cups minced)
  2 cloves garlic, unpeeled
  2 tablespoons butter
  3 tablespoons water
  4 tomatoes, peeled and seeded (3-1/2 cups coarsely chopped)
  2 teaspoons fresh basil leaves _or_
  1 teaspoon dried basil
  1 teaspoon sugar
1/2 teaspoon oregano
1/2 teaspoon salt
    Freshly grated black pepper
 10 colossal pitted black olives, cut flat ends.
 12 anchovy fillets

Dough. Proof yeast in warm water with sugar until foamy. Steel Knife: Place 3/4 cup flour, salt and oil in bowl. Add yeast mixture in 2 batches, turn on/off until mixed -- check consistency. Add more flour as necessary to achieve sticky, not wet, texture. Let machine run 40 seconds to knead dough. Place in oiled bowl, rotate so entire surface is oiled, cover with damp towel, set in warm place (80 degrees) until doubled, about 1 hour. Roll out dough on floured surface, stretching it to fit an 11-inch quiche pan.

Topping. Steel Knife: Mince parsley -- quick on/off turns, set aside. Chop onion, medium coarsemess -- quick on/off turns. Sauté onions and garlic (leave garlic whole, unpeeled and remove before using mixture) in butter and water about 10 minutes, until liquid is absorbed and onions are softened. Spread mixture on unbaked crust. Steel Knife: Chop tomatoes coarsely. Cook over low heat until most of the liquid has cooked away. Add basil, sugar, oregano, salt, pepper to taste. Spoon over onions on crust. Serrated Slicer: Slice olives, using light pressure (see basic techniques). Arrange anchovy fillets (rinse with water to separate, pat dry) in 8 spokes,

(continued on other side)

PISSALADIERE NICOISE (cont.)

overlapping where necessary. Arrange olive slices and 1/2 the minced parsley in sections between spokes. Bake in preheated 400 degree oven for 30 to 35 minutes or until bottom of crust is browned. Sprinkle remaining parsley over baked pizza.

Makes 6 to 8 first-course servings.

BAKED SCALLOPS AUX HERBES

A simple and beautiful presentation of scallops. They should never be overcooked so watch carefully.

```
 3 pounds scallops, sea or bay
 4 tablespoons (1/2 stick) butter
1/4 cup dry white wine
1/2 cup parsley leaves, firmly packed (1/4 cup minced)
 5 tablespoons snipped chives
 1 clove garlic, peeled
 6 shallots, peeled
 2 teaspoons dried basil
 1 teaspoon salt
   Freshly ground black pepper
```

Wash and drain scallops. If using large sea scallops, cut each in 2 or 3 equal slices -- pieces should be as uniform as possible in size. Divide scallops among 8 individual ramekins or a 13-inch gratin dish. Melt the butter, mix with wine.

Steel Knife: Mince parsley and chives together -- quick on/off turns. Set aside 1 tablespoon, stir rest into butter mixture. Mince garlic and shallots -- drop through feed tube with machine running. Mix together with butter mixture. Add seasonings, pour over scallops and cover with foil. The scallops can be prepared up to 4 hours in advance, refrigerated.

Preheat oven to 425 degrees. Bake individual ramekins 10 minutes, gratin dish 20 to 25 minutes or until scallop liquid froths. Watch carefully -- overcooked scallops are tough. Sprinkle with reserved parsley mixture.

Makes 8 servings.

JULIENNED BEET SALAD, MIMOSA

The color contrast of julienned beets on lettuce with a garnish of chopped eggs and parsley is stunning.

```
    Boston lettuce
  1 pound beets, cooked, peeled, cut in largest possible pieces to
    fit feed tube (2 cups julienned)
  1 hard-cooked egg
1/4 cup parsley leaves, firmly packed (1/8 cup minced)
    Mustard Vinaigrette Dressing (recipe follows)
```

Wash and tear Boston lettuce leaves; arrange in large salad bowl. <u>Serrated Slicer</u>: Slice beets, using light pressure. Remove slices from bowl. Holding bowl cover sideways with pusher extended to form a cup, wedge beet slices in base of feed tube so they will not fall out when cover is replaced. Slice, using light pressure; arrange on lettuce leaf.

<u>Steel Knife</u>: Chop egg and parsley together -- quick on/off turns. Sprinkle over beets. Pour Mustard Vinaigrette Dressing over mixture -- toss only when ready to serve.

Makes 8 servings.

MUSTARD VINAIGRETTE DRESSING

```
  1 small clove garlic, peeled
3/4 cup oil (including 2 tablespoons olive oil)
1/4 cup red wine vinegar
  2 teaspoons Dijon mustard
  1 teaspoon salt
    Freshly ground black pepper
```

<u>Steel Knife</u>: Mince garlic -- drop through feed tube while machine is running. Add remaining ingredients -- 3 quick on/off turns.

Makes 1 cup.

VEGETABLE PATE

An original creation. You may substitute your favorite vegetables, provided cooked quantities remain the same. Plunge cooked green vegetables in cold water to preserve the color, then dry them out as taught below. The vegetables can be prepared a day in advance.

```
4-1/2 cups cauliflowerets (large head -- 3-1/2 cups cooked)
1-1/2 pounds carrots, peeled (2 cups cooked, puréed)
    3 ounces green beans (2/3 cup sliced, cooked)
    3 USDA large eggs
    2 teaspoons salt
  1/2 teaspoon freshly granted nutmeg
      Freshly grated black pepper
      Watercress or parsley
```

Cook cauliflowerets in boiling salted water until tender. Drain and dry out moisture in dry pot over medium heat, shaking pan occasionally to prevent burning. Cook carrots until tender; drain and dry out moisture as above. Serrated Slicer: Cut green beans in half (ends removed) to wedge vertically and compactly into feed tube; slice, using medium pressure. Cook 2 minutes in boiling salted water; drain, place in colander under cold running water until cold to the touch to preserve the color (blanching). Dry out moisture as above. Set aside.

Steel Knife: Purée cauliflower -- 6 on/off turns. Add 2 eggs, 1 teaspoon salt, 1/4 teaspoon freshly grated nutmeg and pepper to taste. Let machine run until mixture is puréed. Remove to mixing bowl; add sliced beans and set aside. Purée carrots, cut in thirds -- 6 on/off turns. Add 1 egg, 1 teaspoon salt, 1/4 teaspoon nutmeg and pepper. Let machine run until puréed.

In a buttered 5-cup mold or loaf pan, line bottom with parchment paper, then butter the paper. Layer in cauliflower mixture, wipe sides of mold clean with paper towel -- bang mold to set mixture in place. Layer in carrot mixture. Bang mold down again. Cover dish with buttered foil; set in a bain-marie (water bath), bring to boil on top of the stove, then place in preheated 375 degree oven for 1-1/2 hours. Let rest 10 minutes before inverting on platter. Garnish platter with watercress or parsley.

Makes 8 servings.

TOMATO SAUCE

This sauce is recommended for a green-and-white vegetable pâté combination.

1 can (16 ounces) tomato wedges (1 cup drained)
1 cup half and half
1 teaspoon sugar
1 teaspoon dried basil
  Salt
  Freshly ground black pepper

<u>Steel Knife</u>: Purée drained tomato wedges. Add cream, sugar, basil -- mix well. Transfer to saucepan and cook over low heat until desired consistency, about 10 to 15 minutes. Strain if desired. Serve on the side with Vegetable Pâté.

Makes 1-1/4 cups.

QUICK PAIN DE MIE
(Sandwich Bread)

Quick because it only takes 60 seconds to knead and there are only two risings instead of the traditional three. It can be sliced paper thin for canapés or toast. Not baked in a pain de mie pan*, it has a light texture, characteristic of a conventional white bread.

```
   1 package active dry yeast
 1/2 cup warm water (105 to 115 degrees)
   1 teaspoon sugar
   2 cups unbleached all-purpose flour
   1 cup cake flour
   1 teaspoon salt
 1/2 cup warm milk
   2 tablespoons butter
```

Proof yeast in warm water with sugar. Combine flours and salt. <u>Steel Knife</u>: Place 1-1/2 cups flour mixture in bowl. Add proofed yeast -- 3 on/off turns to blend. Add milk and butter -- repeat on/off turns to blend, then let machine run 5 seconds. Check consistency -- should be very sticky. Add flour only as necessary.

Knead until smooth, not more than 60 seconds. Let rest 5 minutes. Place in oiled bowl, rotate so complete surface is oiled. Cover with damp towel, let double in warm place (80 degrees) about 1 hour. Roll out, fold in thirds, then fold in half the other way. Roll tightly, tuck ends under loaf, pinch seam. Place seam side down in pain de mie pan which has been oiled, cover with damp cloth. Let dough rise almost to top of pan. Cover with oiled lid or baking sheet and bake in preheated 425 degree oven 30 to 35 minutes or until loaf is browned.

This bread will keep for several days.

*A pain de mie pan is a loaf-shaped bread pan with a lid. If baked in an open pan, this recipe will form the conventional rounded loaf. You can improvise your own pain de mie pan by covering a standard loaf pan with a baking sheet, buttered side down and weighted with an ovenproof object.

Makes a 9- or 10-inch loaf.

BOULE DE NEIGE
(Chocolate Snowball)

Another of my very best and most successful desserts.

   8 ounces sweet chocolate, preferably Maillard's, then German
   2 teaspoons undiluted instant coffee
   1 cup sugar
1/2 cup boiling water
   1 cup (2 sticks) unsalted butter (<u>at room temperature</u>), each cut in 6 pieces
   4 USDA large eggs
   1 **tab**lespoon Cognac

Decoration

   1 cup whipping cream
   2 tablespoons sugar
   2 teaspoons Cognac
     Candied violets

Line a 5-cup charlotte mold or soufflé dish with double thickness of foil. Preheat oven to 350 degrees. <u>Steel Knife</u>: Add chocolate, broken into pieces, instant coffee and sugar to work bowl -- turn on/off 4 times to get mixture started, then let machine run until chocolate is finely chopped. With machine running, add boiling water through feed tube. Let machine run until mixture is thoroughly mixed and chocolate is melted. Add butter -- 3 on/off turns. Let machine run until butter is blended completely into chocolate. Add eggs, Cognac. Let machine run 10 seconds.

Empty mixture into prepared mold; bake in preheated oven 40 minutes until a thick crust has formed on top. The mixture will recede as it cools. Let cool. Wrap airtight and refrigerate. Will keep up to 2 weeks and can also be frozen.

<u>To serve</u>. Peel off foil (mixture will look sticky and irregular). Whip cream until thick with electric beater, sweeten and flavor. Fill pastry bag fitted with a medium size star tube; cover mold completely with rosettes so no chocolate shows. Decorate top and sides with candied violets. Chill until served. Cut in small slices.

Makes 8 to 12 servings.

SLICED PINEAPPLE IN KIRSCH

A low-calorie option for the calorie watchers who have to resist the Boule de Neige.

1 fresh pineapple, about 3-1/2 pounds (2-1/2 cups sliced)
4 tablespoons Kirsch
  Zest of 1 orange

Cut pineapple in half lengthwise through the leaf. Carefully remove pineapple fruit from shell in lengthwise quarter sections, not cutting through the shell which will be the serving dish. Cut off core; cut quarters crosswise in half so they will fit in feed tube.

Serrated Slicer: Slice pineapple, using medium pressure. Mix with Kirsch and orange zest -- refrigerate. Spoon fruit back into shells to serve.

Makes 6 servings.

NOTES

BASIC RECIPES

Basic Mayonnaise

Basic Vinaigrette

Crème Fraiche

Lemon Curd

Pâte Brisée for Quiches

Pâte Sucreé for Dessert Tarts

Vanilla Sauce

BASIC MAYONNAISE

    1 USDA large egg
    1 teaspoon fresh lemon juice
    1 teaspoon red wine vinegar
    1 teaspoon Dijon mustard
    1 teaspoon salt
      Freshly ground white pepper
1-1/2 cups oil (any oil of choice -- my favorite,
      safflower with 3 tablespoons olive oil)

<u>Steel Knife</u>: Combine egg, lemon juice, vinegar, mustard, salt, pepper and 3 tablespoons oil in bowl. Turn machine on/off 4 times to blend and slightly thicken mixture. With machine running, pour oil in thin, steady stream through feed tube until mayonnaise thickens. Add remaining oil more quickly. Adjust seasoning to taste.

Makes about 1-3/4 cups.

BASIC VINAIGRETTE

3/4 cup oil
1/4 cup red wine vinegar
  1 teaspoon salt
    Freshly ground black pepper

<u>Plastic Knife</u>: Mix all ingredients; pour over salad ingredients and toss to coat evenly. Taste and adjust seasonings.

Makes 1 cup.

CREME FRAICHE

1/2 pint sour cream
1 pint heavy or whipping cream

Combine sour and heavy creams in heavy saucepan; heat very slowly and carefully so that mixture is barely warm, not at all hot (that would stop fermentation). Pour into jar, cover partially, leave at room temperature overnight or longer, until mixture is thickened. Mix well, cover tightly; refrigerate.

Makes about 2 cups.

LEMON CURD

This lemon curd is deliberately tart to preserve the lemon flavor in the various fillings for which it is used.

Zest of 2 large lemons
2/3 cup sugar
5 USDA large egg yolks
Juice of 2 large lemons (about 1/2 cup)
1/2 cup (1 stick) unsalted butter, melted

Steel Knife: Mince lemon zest with sugar -- 4 on/off turns, then let machine run until zest is of desired fineness. Add egg yolks and lemon juice -- let machine run 5 seconds to blend. With machine running, pour melted butter through feed tube.

Pour mixture into heavy stainless steel saucepan or stainless top of a double boiler. Cook very slowly, mixing constantly with a stainless wire whisk or wooden spoon until thickened. Cool. Lemon curd will keep in a covered jar, refrigerated for 2 to 3 months.

Makes 1-2/3 cups.

PATE BRISEE FOR QUICHES
(partially baked crust)

1-1/2 cups unbleached all-purpose flour
  1/2 teaspoon salt
    1 USDA large egg yolk
    4 ounces (1 stick) chilled unsalted butter,
      cut in 6 pieces
    5 tablespoons ice water

Steel Knife: Place flour, salt, egg yolk and butter in bowl. Turn machine on/off until mixture resembles coarse meal. With machine running, pour ice water through feed tube -- stop machine once dough is in a ball. Remove dough, press flat, wrap in plastic and chill at least 2 hours. Roll out on lightly floured board, place in buttered 11-inch quiche pan, prick bottom and sides with a fork, refrigerate 30 minutes or until firm. Line with parchment paper, fill with beans or rice, bake in preheated 400 degree oven 12 minutes. Remove paper and beans, prick crust again, bake 6 minutes longer or until crust is lightly browned. This will produce a crisp crust that resists moisture.

Makes an 11-inch crust.

PATE SUCREE FOR DESSERT TARTS
(completely baked crust)

1-1/2 cups unbleached all-purpose flour
    2 tablespoons sugar
      Pinch salt
    1 USDA large egg yolk
    4 ounces (1 stick) chilled unsalted butter,
      cut in 6 pieces
    5 tablespoons ice water

Steel Knife: Place flour, sugar, salt and egg yolk in bowl. Turn machine on/off until mixture resembles coarse meal. With machine running, pour ice water through feed tube. Once dough forms a ball, remove, press flat, wrap in plastic, chill at least 2 hours. Roll out on lightly floured board, place in lightly buttered 11-inch quiche pan or flan, prick bottom and sides with a fork; refrigerate 30 minutes. Line with parchment paper, fill with beans or rice, bake in preheated 400 degree oven 12 minutes. Remove paper and beans, prick crust again, bake 10 minutes longer or until crust is well baked and browned. Watch carefully so it doesn't burn. Let cool on wire rack.

Makes an 11-inch crust.

VANILLA SAUCE

1 cup sour cream
4 tablespoons Greek vanilla syrup (softened)*
  or
3 tablespoons confectioners sugar
1 teaspoon vanilla
1 inch vanilla bean, split and scraped

Plastic Knife: Combine sour cream with Greek vanilla syrup or confectioners sugar, vanilla and seeds from vanilla bean -- on/off turns only until combined; chill.

*Available at specialty food stores.

Makes about 1-1/4 cups.

INDEX

Appetizers and Hors d'Oeuvre
  Chinese Lettuce Appetizers, 59
  Crème de Camembert, 13
  Eggs Cressonière, 49
  Fish Pâté au Cresson, 77
  French Country Pâté, 48
  Green Onion Quiche, 30
  Gravlax, 8
  Hummous, 76
  Mushroom Salad, 24
  Onion Parmesan Appetizers, 88
  Pissaladière Nicoise, 89
  Salmon Pâté, 67
  Scallops, Marinated, 18
  Spinach-Feta Strudel, 38
  Tapenade, 19
  Taramosalada, 39
Apricot Mousse in Orange Shells, 63
Baked Eggs and Cheese aux Herbes, 10
Baked Scallops aux Herbes, 91
Basic Recipes
  Crème Fraîche, 101
  Lemon Curd, 101
  Mayonnaise, 100
  Pâte Brisée for Quiches, 102
  Pâte Sucrée for Dessert Tarts, 102
  Vanilla Sauce, 103
  Vinaigrette, 100
Beef with Broccoli, Water Chestnuts and Mushrooms, 58
Blueberry and Peach Crêpes, 15
Boule de Neige, 96
Breads
  Cheese, 53
  Classic American Coffee Cake, 16
  French, 27
  French Brioche, 11
  Pain Complet, 82
  Quick Pain de Mie, 95
  Wheat Germ, 44
  Whole Wheat, 82
Broiled Tarragon Chicken Breasts, 50
Cakes
  Chocolate Torte, 55
  Classic American Coffee Cake, 16
  French Cream Cheese Cake, Strawberry Sauce, 83
Caper Mayonnaise Salad, 52
Carrot and Turnip Purée, 32

Cauliflower, Radish, Green Pepper Slaw, 34
Cheese
  Baked Eggs and Cheese, aux Herbes, 10
  Bread, 53
  Crème de Camembert, 13
  Spinach-Feta Strudel, 38
Chinese
  Lettuce Appetizers, 59
  Noodles Supreme, 61
Chocolate Torte, 55
Clafouti, Mixed Fruit, 85
Classic American Coffee Cake, 16
Condiment Tray, 71
Cookies
  Sablés, 64
Courgettes Rapées (Shredded Zucchini), 23
Crème de Camembert, 13
Crème Fraîche, 101
Crêpes
  Peach and Blueberry Crêpes, 15
Cucumber
  à la Grecque, 81
  Yogurt Salad, 72
Desserts
  Apricot Mousse in Orange Shells, 63
  Blueberry and Peach Crêpes, 15
  Boule de Neige, 96
  Chocolate Torte, 55
  Classic American Coffee Cake, 16
  French Cream Cheese Cake, Strawberry Sauce, 83
  Fresh Strawberry Tart, 73
  German Apple Pancake, 14
  La Tarte Tatin, 25
  Lemon Cream Puffs, 35
  Mixed Fruit Clafouti, 85
  Peach and Blueberry Crêpes, 15
  Sablés, 64
  Sliced Oranges Grand Marnier, Strawberry Sauce, 45
  Sliced Pineapple in Kirsch, 97
Eggs
  Baked Eggs and Cheese aux Herbes, 10
  Eggs Cressonière, 49
  Green Onion Quiche, 30
Eggplant and Rice, Tian of, 80
Fish and Seafood
  Fish Pâté au Cresson, 77
  Gravlax (Swedish Marinated Salmon), 8
  Salmon Pâté, 67

Fish and Seafood (cont.)
  Scallops
    Baked aux Herbes, 91
    Marinated, with Green Mayonnaise, 18
  Stuffed Fish en Papillote, 31
  Tapenade, 19
  Taramosalada, 39
French Bread, 27
French Brioche Bread, 11
French Country Pâté, 48
French Cream Cheese Cake, 83
Fresh Strawberry Tart, 73
Fruit
  Blueberry and Peach Crêpes, 15
  Condiment Tray, 71
  Fresh Strawberry Preserves, 12
  La Tarte Tatin, 25
  Lemon Cream Puffs, 35
  Mixed Fruit Clafouti, 85
  Sliced Oranges Grand Marnier, Strawberry Sauce, 45
  Sliced Pineapple in Kirsch, 97
  Strawberry Tart, 73
German Apple Pancake, 14
Gravlax (Swedish Marinated Salmon), 8
Green Onion Quiche, 30
Green Pepper, Radish, Cauliflower Salad, 34
Greek Salad, 43
Green Mayonnaise, 18
Herbed
  Tomatoes, 20
  Leg of Lamb, 79
Hors d'Oeuvre (see Appetizers)
Hummous, 76
Japanese Relish, 62
Julienned Beet Salad, Mimosa, 92
La Tarte Tatin, 25
Lamb
  Curry, 69
  Herbed Leg of, 79
  Shish Kebabs, Lemon, 40
Lemon
  Cream Puffs, 35
  Curd, 101
  Shish Kebabs, 40
Lentil, Red or Orange Relish, 72
Marinated Scallops, Green Mayonnaise, 18
Matchstick Potatoes, 33
Mayonnaise
  au Cresson, 77
  Basic, 100
  Caper, 52
  Green, 18
  Mustard, 9

Meat
  Beef with Broccoli, Water Chestnuts and Mushrooms, 58
  Chinese Noodles Supreme, 61
  Herbed Leg of Lamb, 79
  French Country Pâté, 48
  Lamb Curry, 69
  Lemon Shish Kebabs, 40
  Moussaka, 41
  Stuffed Breast of Veal, 21
Mixed Fruit Clafouti, 85
Moussaka, 41
Mousse, Apricot, 63
Mushroom Endive Salad, 24
Mustard Mayonnaise, 9
Noodles Supreme, Chinese, 61
Onion Parmesan Appetizers, 88
Oranges Grand Marnier, Strawberry Sauce, 45
Pain Complet, 82
Pain de Mie, Quick, 95
Pancake, German Apple, 14
Pastry (see Pies)
Pâte
  Brisée for Quiches, 102
  Sucrée for Dessert Tarts, 102
Pâté
  Fish, au Cresson, 77
  French Country, 48
  Salmon, 67
  Vegetable, 93
Peach and Blueberry Crêpes, 15
Pies and Pastries
  Entrée
    Baked Eggs and Cheese aux Herbes, 10
    Green Onion Quiche, 30
  Dessert
    La Tarte Tatin, 25
    Lemon Cream Puffs, 35
    Strawberry Tart, 73
Pineapple, Sliced in Kirsch, 97
Pissaladière Nicoise (French Pizza), 89
Pizza, French (Pissaladière Nicoise), 89
Poultry
  Broiled Tarragon Chicken Breasts, 50
  Chinese Lettuce Appetizers, 59
Preserves, Fresh Strawberry, 12
Quiche, Green Onion, 30
Radish, Cauliflower, Green Pepper Slaw, 34
Red or Orange Lentil Relish, 72
Relish
  Japanese, 62
  Red or Orange Lentil, 72

Rice
  Saffron, 68
  Tian of Eggplant and, 80
Sablés, 64
Saffron Rice, 68
Salad Dressings
  Mayonnaise
    au Cresson, 77
    Basic, 100
    Caper, 52
    Green, 18
    Mustard, 9
  Vinaigrette
    Basic, 100
    Basil, 51
    Mustard, 92
Salads
  Cauliflower, Radish, Green Pepper Slaw, 34
  Condiment Tray, 71
  Cucumber
    à la Grecque, 81
    Yogurt, 72
  Greek, 43
  Japanese Relish, 62
  Julienned Beet, Mimosa, 92
  Mushroom Endive, 24
  Tomatoes, Herbed, 20
  Tomatoes, Sliced with Basil Vinaigrette, 51
Salmon Pâté, 67
Sauces
  Strawberry, 83
  Tomato, 94
  Vanilla, 103
Scallops
  Baked aux Herbes, 91
  Marinated, with Green Mayonnaise, 18
Seafood (see Fish)
Soup, Zucchini and Tomato, 66
Spinach-Feta Strudel, 38
Strawberry
  Preserves, Fresh, 12
  Sauce, 83
  Tart, Fresh, 73
Stuffed Breast of Veal, 21
Stuffed Fish en Papillote, 31
Stuffings and Forcemeats
  Stuffed Breast of Veal, 21
  Stuffed Fish en Papillote, 31
Tapenade, 19
Taramosalada, 39

Tian of Eggplant and Rice, 80
Tomato Sauce, 94
Tomatoes
   Herbed, 20
   Sliced, Basil Vinaigrette, 51
   and Zucchini Soup, 66
Turnip and Carrot Purée, 32
Veal, Stuffed Breast of, 21
Vegetable Pâté, 93
Vegetables
   Carrot and Turnip Purée, 32
   Courgettes Rapées (Shredded Zucchini), 23
   Eggplant and Rice, Tian of, 80
   Hummous, 76
   Japanese Relish, 62
   Matchstick Potatoes, 33
   Moussaka, 41
   Spinach-Feta Strudel, 38
   Tian of Eggplant and Rice, 80
   Tomatoes, Herbed, 20
   Vegetable Pâté, 93
   Zucchini, Shredded (Courgettes Rapées), 23
Vanilla Sauce, 103
Vinaigrette
   Basic, 100
   Basil, 51
   Mustard, 92
Wheat Germ Bread, 44
Yogurt Cucumber Salad, 72
Zucchini
   and Tomato Soup, 66
   Shredded, 23

NOTES

NOTES

NOTES